Standards-Based

Activities and Assessments
for the
Differentiated Classroom

By
Carolyn Coil

Pieces of Learning

© 2004 Pieces of Learning
CLC0309
ISBN 978-1-931334-28-0
www.piecesoflearning.com
Printed by McNaughton & Gunn, Inc.
Saline, MI USA
05/2010

Table of Contents

123241

Acknowledgements

Many thanks to Kathy Balsamo, Stan Balsamo and Peggy Hord at Pieces of Learning both for their encouragement and for giving me deadlines. This book would not be finished without them!

Special thanks to Nancy Polette, my friend and colleague who wrote the Landforms poems.

Thanks to all of the teachers in my classes and in my workshops over the years who have inspired me and given me many wonderful ideas. Many of the ideas and activities in this book began with the teachers I have worked with.

Thank you to Christopher Wells for his patience in teaching me the basics of Microsoft® Word that I needed to write this book.

Thank you to Sally Krisel, coordinator of gifted, State of Georgia, for sparking my creativity about standards and extensions.

Finally, a most special thanks to my wonderful husband Doug who encourages me in all I do, carries boxes of books for me and understands when I bury myself in my office for days on end in order to get a book finished!

Dedication

To my three beautiful grandchildren

- Jason Coil
- Kaylee Coil
- Ainsley Coil

in hopes that your future teachers will recognize your individual gifts, abilities and talents, encourage and help you when you struggle, and see each of you as a special child of God.

Index by Topics

Index by Standards

It has been my experience in working with teachers that nearly all know the standards to teach. Most carry around a grade level or subject area list of standards constantly! They make reference to the standards almost as often as they open their plan books. Some are required to write the standards on the board each day; nearly all write them in their lesson plans.

One problem for me in writing a book for teachers working in many different states throughout the United States and in other locations throughout the world is that the standards aren't standardized! I cannot choose one set of standards and apply them to every grade level in every location. For that reason, I have indexed the activities by subject area, assuming that most of the activities in a particular unit would apply to standards in a given subject.

However, the activities in this book are integrated across the curriculum. Many of them are interdisciplinary. Most require reading, writing, gathering information, organizing and/or research skills. Therefore, many of the activities that I have categorized in one category may address the standards in other areas as well.

Use this Index as a beginning point. Then use the form on page 10 to correlate your own standards to the activities and assessments in this book.

The Standard is.... Language Arts

The Standard is ... Math

The Standard is ... Science

The Standard is ... Social Studies

The Standard is ... Health

The Standard is ... Visual/Performing Arts

- Other (visual and performing arts are included in almost every set of activities in this book)

Introduction

Differentiation, assessment and standards-based learning are major buzz words and prime areas of concern for those of us working in education today. Teachers and administrators are well aware that all of their students need to meet the standards, yet at the same time they are equally well aware that students come to them at very different ability and readiness levels, with different interests, intelligences, learning styles and learning modalities.

Thus, the need for differentiation is obvious to most educators. Therefore, the challenge of differentiation doesn't come in identifying the need. Instead, it comes as teachers work to put the theory into practice in their classrooms. This book is written to address this challenge and provide a link between the theory and the **"how-to" of differentiation.**

Who Needs This Book?

First and foremost, this is a book for **teachers**. I have discovered that while most teachers would like to differentiate their curriculum and day-to-day instruction, many do not understand how to actually implement differentiation. They need practical strategies that are user-friendly and that do not take an inordinate amount of time to plan and put into practice. Teachers also need ways to assess and grade the variety of student projects and performances that are often the result of differentiated instruction.

If you are a teacher new to differentiation, this book provides you with many examples of activities and assessments you can use as you begin to differentiate your curriculum. Utilize the examples as they are written or use them as models for writing your own. When teachers take the first step in differentiating the curriculum, other steps generally follow as they become more comfortable with this type of teaching.

If you are already differentiating your instruction, use this book to gain new ideas for both student activities and ways to assess products, performances, and outcomes. Assessing a variety of products and performances is never easy, and writing assessment criteria succinctly is difficult, even for many experienced teachers. This book gives you new ideas for student products as well as ideas and wording for writing the corresponding assessment criteria.

Administrators and **program coordinators** also need this book. It offers many practical strategies that you can share with your teachers during a faculty meeting, short in-service session, or study group. It will help you translate the theory into classroom practice and will give you a multitude of different examples suitable for all grade levels.

Why I Wrote This Book

In my staff development workshops, I share somewhere between ten and fifteen strategies for differentiation. Three of the most popular are the Tic-Tac-Toe format, the *Teaching Tools* Individual Lesson Plan format, and the Tiered Unit/Lesson Plan. Even though I show teachers how to write their own lessons and units in each of these formats, and give workshop time for them to do this, many teachers have asked me if I would create some of these **differentiated activities with corresponding assessments** for them.

This request, which I have heard from teachers over and over again, was the genesis for this book. It contains 24 Tic-Tac-Toe activities and assessments, 10 *Teaching Tools* Individual

8

<u>Lesson Plans</u> and assessments, and 15 <u>Tiered Lessons or Units</u> with assessments. They are already written and ready to use! Teachers can use them, modify them, adapt them, or take ideas from them and write their own using the *Activities and Assessments* CD.

How To Use This Book

This book is organized into sections and then alphabetically by topic. The <u>Tic-Tac-Toe</u> activity grids are alphabetized by topic, as are the *Teaching Tools* <u>Individual Lesson Plans</u> and the <u>Tiered Lesson Plans</u>. Most are appropriate for grades 3-9, though there are a few targeted for early elementary and several for high school students.

Find the topic or subjects that most closely match the topics and units you are teaching. Check to make sure the activities seem appropriate for your grade level. Look at **your standards** and correlate them with the activities and assessments you have picked. Use the form on page 10 to record the topics and your standards.

You may copy any of the activities and assessments in this book to use directly with students in your classroom. You are encouraged to change or adapt the activities and assessments to meet the specific needs of your students, your curriculum, or your state standards. The *Activities and Assessments* CD allows you to download any of the activities and assessments in this book and in WORD format to write your own <u>Tic-Tac-Toe</u> activities, *Teaching Tools* <u>Individual Lesson Plans</u>, and <u>Tiered Lesson Plans</u>.

At the end of each section of this book you will find a set of step-by-step guidelines for writing your own differentiated activities and assessments using the format featured in that particular section. In each case, there are blank forms for you to use, and they are also included on the *Activities and Assessments* CD. After you have tried some of the examples, challenge yourself to write a differentiated unit or lesson of your own!

I hope this book encourages all teachers to try differentiation. I further hope it will truly be a timesaver for the many teachers who are already differentiating their instruction but do not have the planning time to develop all of the differentiated activities they would like to have.

Using this book both as a timesaver and as a guide in implementing differentiation should result in a richer curriculum and more exciting learning opportunities for all students.

Standards:

_____

_____

Name or Number of Activity/Topic   **Page Number**

_____   _____

_____   _____

_____   _____

_____   _____

_____   _____

_____   _____

_____   _____

Standards:

_____

_____

Name or Number of Activity/Topic   **Page Number**

_____   _____

_____   _____

_____   _____

_____   _____

_____   _____

_____   _____

Differentiation: An Overview

Ms. Garner looked at her 4th grade class. Each student was truly a unique individual, yet she basically taught all of them the same content using the same strategies, as if they were clones of each other. Under extreme pressure to teach all her students the 4th grade standards, she could think of no other approach to make sure they all learned what they were supposed to learn. A few of them responded well to this approach, but many were bored, and others seemed to be falling further behind. She knew she should meet individual needs, but she didn't know how to begin. "There are so many of them and only one of me!" she thought ruefully.

Differentiated Curriculum: What is it?

Like Ms. Garner, many teachers are frustrated with the traditional "one size fits all" approach to teaching. At one point in time, "teaching to the middle" may have been a workable strategy, but as the *big* middle has become the *little* middle in most classrooms, teachers are increasingly seeking ways to diversify and differentiate their instruction.

The concept of differentiated curriculum originated in the field of gifted education. Public Law 91-230, the federal law establishing a definition of gifted and talented students, states:

> *"These are students who require differentiated educational programs and/or services beyond those normally provided by regular school programs in order to realize their contributions to themselves and society."*

In many school districts, the impetus for differentiation starts when teachers and administrators look for ways to meet the needs of gifted students. They soon realize that this is a philosophy that works for **all students**. Differentiation for students with disabilities and for students for whom English is a second language is appropriate, too. Indeed, for many teachers, it becomes their basic teaching method and style.

Differentiated curriculum moves teachers away from the "one size fits all" curriculum that really fits no one! It encourages students to become more responsible for their own learning and to recognize and use their own strengths, thereby helping them become lifelong autonomous learners.

Brain research done in the past decade reveals much about how humans learn and provides another reason for differentiating curriculum. Briefly, researchers concur that learning occurs when the brain seeks connections to what it already knows. These connections form differently for each person because each person's experiences are different. Our brains are individualized, and our learning experiences need to be, too! Differentiating curriculum is an approach to teaching that works well in helping us reach this goal.

Differentiation is based on the premise that students learn in different ways; therefore, we must provide them with a number of different options for learning. Furthermore, students come to us with different skill levels and content knowledge, so they are at dissimilar entry points in terms of learning when they come into the classroom on the first day of school. Differentiation helps us tailor our instruction as we consider each student's interests, level of readiness, pace of learning, learning styles and modalities, strengths and weaknesses, and types of intelligences.

Differentiated curriculum provides students with several different options for learning. It includes:

1. Different ways to learn the information

2. Different amounts of time to complete work

3. Different approaches to learning because of cultural background or language acquisition

4. Different levels of learning

5. Different assignments for students in the same classroom

6. Different means to assess what has been learned

Let's examine each of these in more detail:

1. Students learn in a variety of different ways. Using learning theories such as learning modalities, learning styles and multiple intelligences to form the base for curricular planning helps us differentiate for a wide variety of learners. Additionally, brain-based approaches to curriculum usually address a wide range of learning needs. Both the Tic-Tac-Toe activities and the *Teaching Tools* Individual Lesson Plans will help you differentiate in this way.

2. As every teacher knows, students who are doing exactly the same assignment finish it at different times. If you've planned a half hour for a certain task, one student will finish in five minutes while another will have barely begun when the time is up. Planning what you will do with both the slower student and the one who works at a rapid pace is an important skill in differentiating curriculum. You want to make sure both students are mastering the standards. At the same time, you don't want the student who finishes quickly to do more of the same work without learning anything new. One of the many uses for lessons and units in this book is as anchoring activities for faster students. These are ongoing independent tasks that students can move to automatically when they have complet-ed or compacted out of regular classroom assignments. In this book you will find higher level thinking activities students can work on when they finish the assigned work or when they demonstrate their mastery of skills or standards. For slower students, pick the most essential activities for standards mastery.

3. The United States has always been a country of diverse cultures. However, in the past decade we have had more ESL students than ever before from diverse cultures and for whom English is not their first language. This creates new challenges for teachers both in terms of helping these students with language acquisition and stardards mastery while learning to understand the many cultures from which they come. Including a variety of cultural viewpoints and examples within the curriculum and throughout daily instruction will help in differentiating for these students. Furthermore, emphasizing activities that utilize visual and kinesthetic learning while helping these students in language acquisition is a good strategy for differentiation. Many of the activities and lessons in this book can be used to differentiate instruction for Limited English Proficient (LEP/ESL) students.

4. Students can work on the same standards but at different levels of thinking and intensity. Some students will just barely understand a concept or idea while others can explore it with a great deal of depth and complexity. When you plan lessons and units reflecting these levels of thinking, you can appropriately target your lessons to meet the needs of all students. Bloom's Taxonomy provides one structure for planning ways to teach students who are at different levels of learning. Tiering lessons and units is another good approach for differentiating in this way. You will find a number of Tiered Units in this book as well as step-by-step guidelines for writing your own. You will also find activities using Bloom's Taxonomy both in the *Teaching Tools* Individualized Lesson Plans and in the Tic-Tac-Toe activities.

5. In a differentiated classroom, the assumption should be that sometimes everyone will be doing the same work, but many times this will not be the case. Instead, students in the same classroom will be working on different assignments. Teachers need to plan carefully for this, because they need to know which students are doing which activities and because students need to know exactly what they are supposed to be doing and what guidelines they need to follow. Clear and precise assessment criteria plays an important role when students are doing different assignments. Equally important is informing the parents how, when and why their children will be doing assignments that are not the same for everyone. Activities and units in this book give students choices in the different assignments they are to do. Use the record keeper on page 83 to keep track of which students are doing which assignments.

6. If you differentiate your curriculum and instruction appropriately, it seems logical that you should also differentiate assessments. This may appear to be a strange concept in this era of standardized assessment and testing. Nevertheless, in a differentiated classroom setting, all students can be working toward the same standards but in different ways. This means you should assess individual projects, products and performances according to the standards but based on agreed-upon criteria that may not be the same for every student. Some students can work on extensions to the basic criteria while others may strive mightily just to master the basics. This is OK! In this book you will find suggested assessment criteria for every unit and every activity. You can modify the assessment as you see fit, eliminating some of the criteria or adding more. The number of points for each of the assessment criteria is not assigned. This decision is yours. However, this book gives you a place to start in assessing the large variety of products and performances that students may complete in a differentiated classroom setting.

Important Concepts in Differentiation

Four important concepts for differentiated instruction are:

• **Flexibility** – A flexible mindset is absolutely essential for anyone who wants to differentiate instruction. An attitude of *"I'll try something new and see how it works"* is a good start. On the other hand, a teacher who says, *"I've always taught this unit in the same way, and I'm not changing now!"* is probably not a good candidate for differentiation.

• **Resources** – Differentiated curriculum requires using a wide variety of resources. It is quite a change from having every student using one book and working on the same page! These resources do not need to be costly. In fact, most teachers and most schools already have the resources. It usually is a matter of locating, organizing, separating and choosing which ones to use. Make a commitment to yourself to spend a day going through your supplemental books and your files. You will be amazed at how many resources you already have! Enlist your school media specialist to help you find the resources you need for a differentiated unit or lesson.

• **Planning** – Like all good teaching, differentiation takes planning. Beyond looking at the curriculum and the grade level standards, teachers who differentiate must also look at the learning needs of individual students. Planning often involves using pre-assessment and formative assessments to find out what students already know. This book features three easy-to-use planning models that work well in differentiating classroom instruction. Use the examples from this book, but also use these models to help you plan your own units of work.

• **Choices** – Differentiation typically involves giving students some choice in their learning activities. This does not mean giving students unlimited or unstructured choices. It does mean having a set of possible learning activities from which students will be able to choose at least some of the time. I am passionate about the value of learning, so I feel strongly that students should never be sitting in class doing nothing. Learning time is just too important! For this reason, my basic rule about student choices is: **The one choice you never have is the choice to do nothing.**

Approaches to Differentiation

There are four major strategies to deal with content when you decide to differentiate. Any or all of these approaches may be appropriate, depending on the needs of your students, the content you are teaching, and your classroom situation. Often teachers combine several of these as they plan differentiated instruction.

1. Acceleration - This approach moves students vertically through the curriculum at a faster pace. To do this successfully, teachers usually have to work with teachers at higher grade levels. Some students may arrive in your classroom already accelerated. It is important to find out what they already know so that you can proceed from that point.

2. Enrichment - This strategy usually incorporates studying topics not included in the regular curriculum. Students may have an interest in certain areas of study, and enrichment allows them to study these in more depth. Enrichment also includes exposing students to a wide variety of interesting ideas and concepts through guest speakers, mini-classes, etc.

14

3. Extensions – This approach uses activities tied to the regular curriculum but expand or broaden it in some way. Students explore facets of the unit in greater depth and often share what they have learned with the rest of the class. Many of the activities in this book include extensions.

4. Remediation – Most students develop academic holes as they go through school. These are concepts, skills or knowledge that they should have learned but for some reason did not. The need for remediation is widespread. It can be seen in gifted and talented students as well as struggling students. When academic holes are discovered, they need to be dealt with quickly so that further learning is not hindered.

Beginning Steps and Challenges in Differentiating Curriculum

The need for differentiation is obvious. All teachers would like to accommodate each child and meet each of their diverse needs. How to actually **do** the differentiation is the major concern of teachers. Without practical, easy-to-implement strategies, most teachers go back to teaching in the "one size fits all" mode. Therefore, it is essential to become familiar with at least one differentiation strategy that makes sense and start there.

Being able to differentiate curriculum requires that teachers be very familiar and comfortable with the curriculum they teach. Thus, differentiation is more difficult for beginning teachers who are becoming acquainted with and teaching their curriculum for the first time. It is almost as difficult for an experienced teacher who is teaching a different grade level or subject for the first time. If you are teaching something new, begin by trying to differentiate just one lesson or unit and build from there.

Planning differentiated activities and developing assessments for them takes time. This book helps teachers with this challenge. There are many activities and assessments already planned, developed and ready-to-use. Feel free to use them exactly as they are written or adapt them to meet your needs. Additionally, the activities and assessments will provide patterns for you to use as you write your own. The customizable CD makes planning and writing them easier for you.

I hope this book provides you with many ideas as you look for ways to differentiate your instruction, your curriculum, and your assessments. Focus on both the standards and on the needs of your students as you journey down the path of differentiation.

Differentiated Curriculum and Assessment: Two Concepts that go Hand-in-Hand

It is almost impossible to talk about differentiated curriculum and instruction without also discussing assessment issues. Assessment plays a significant role in differentiation, from showing us what students have already mastered to helping us develop and present to them the appropriate level of work. Good assessments can assist us in charting student progress and in helping students see what they have learned and what they need to learn next.

On another level, assessment can sometimes be a stumbling block to differentiation. Teachers must consider grades and want to be fair in grading all students. If students are given a choice of activities, how is it possible to grade them in any standardized way? How can one teacher possibly develop alternative or performance assessments for a large variety of student activities? These are legitimate questions. This book attempts to answer these concerns.

3 Types of Assessments Helpful in Differentiating Instruction

There are three major types of assessments that one can use in the differentiated classroom. To be useful, all three must be aligned with curricular and instructional objectives and with state standards. The three types are:

- Pre-assessments

- Formative assessments

- Summative assessments

Most of the assessments in this book can be used as formative assessments, summative assessments, or both. However, pre-assessment is usually done via a pretest, student observation, a checklist or some other evidence of past work and knowledge.

Pre-assessment ...

- is any method, strategy or process used to determine a student's current level of readiness or interest in order to plan for appropriate instruction.

- provides data and information that can determine learning options or levels for students in a differentiated classroom.

- helps teachers understand the nature of learning differences in his/her students before planning instruction.

- allows students to demonstrate mastery or to show where remediation might be needed before instruction begins.

Formative Assessment ...

• is the process of accumulating information about a student's progress to help make **ongoing instructional decisions** during a unit of work.

• alerts the teacher early on about student misconceptions or lack of understanding about what is being studied.

• allows students to build on what they already know.

• provides regular feedback to students.

• provides evidence of progress in learning over time.

• gives teachers information about what their students already know (or don't know) so they can change, modify or extend the instructional activities in which students are engaged. Teachers can use this information to make adjustments to their instruction as they teach and can differentiate instruction accordingly. It is assessment **for** learning rather than assessment **of** learning.

Summative Assessment ...

• is a means to determine a student's **mastery** of information, knowledge, skills, concepts, etc. after the unit or learning activity has been completed.

• should parallel the formative assessments that were used during the learning process.

• may determine an exit grade or score and can be tied to a final decision about a student.

• should align with instructional/curricular objectives, standards, and benchmarks.

• may be a form of alternative assessment; doesn't always have to be a test.

• Find out what a student knows, understands, and can do before you begin teaching. Use observations and open-ended questions as well as formal pretests of subject content.

• Make sure you and the students know the goals they are working toward before they begin working. Goals should not be a moving target. Students should clearly know when they have accomplished a goal. When students see they can accomplish a small task or goal successfully, they are more likely to attempt the next step.

• Use ongoing classroom assessments to build your students' confidence in themselves as learners.

• Make assessment criteria explicit by using rubrics or checklists.

• Different student products and performances require different types of assessment criteria. Make sure your students are clear about the criteria and expectations, especially when everyone in the class is not doing the same activity.

• Develop observational checklists to document what you are seeing in the classroom.

• Give continuous formal and informal feedback to students as well as suggestions about how to improve. Assessment should not be a mystery and should not be done just for points or grades!

• Adjust your instruction based on the ongoing assessment of your students. Don't make students continue to practice skills or complete busywork once they have mastered the information.

• When individual students have mastered the concepts or standards being taught, allow them to work on alternate enrichment or extension activities.

• Foster thinking-about-thinking (metacognition) by asking students not only **what** they learned from the activity but also **how** they learned it.

• Design ways students can continuously communicate with teachers and parents about their progress. This should happen often, not just at report card time.

• When you use summative assessments, make sure they relate to the formative assessments the students have done. Items on the final test should be no surprise to students who have done well on the formative assessments along the way.

Assessments in This Book

One of the biggest questions teachers have about giving students a variety of different choices in learning activities is the problem of how to grade them. When I first tackled this problem, I thought the best approach was to develop full and complex rubrics for every student activity. While that may theoretically be the best approach, it simply is not practical in the real world of school! Teachers do not have the time to develop so many different rubrics — and in some schools they don't even have the copy paper available to copy them if they did!

Some student activities should be accompanied by a complete and well-defined rubric. For more information about how to develop this type of rubric and for 134 rubrics that are already written for you, see _Solving the Assessment Puzzle_, Pieces of Learning, publisher.

But what about assessing student products when students have eight or nine or twelve choices of different activities? Is it possible to develop useful assessments when this is the case? I believe it can be done using shorter checklist-type assessment indicators that will fit into a small block of space (like the square on a Tic-Tac-Toe grid). Such assessments are the basis of this book.

There are several keys in writing these shorter assessments:

• Use a checklist format, making sure you have assessment indicators for all the important aspects of the product or performance.

• Use product criteria cards as a shortcut to indicate quality expectations for the product itself.

• Highlight the important parts of the content in the criteria checklist.

• Make sure the assessment criteria are correlated to the standards you are teaching.

• Include extensions when possible to challenge higher ability students.

Product Criteria Cards: An Assessment Shortcut

Another major concern teachers have about project and performance assessment is how to develop fair and clear assessment criteria without making the list of requirements too long and without overly emphasizing product over content. One way to handle this matter is to use Product Criteria Cards. These cards can be used over and over again every time a student does the same (or a similar) product.

You may have the same generic criteria for certain products or performances your students engage in regardless of the specific academic content they cover. The same may be true within a grade level or an academic department. When this is the case, consider developing Product Criteria Cards to use every time students do the same type of product — regardless of the content. When all students know and understand the criteria for certain products and have Product Criteria Cards readily available for reference, assessment becomes much easier for you and more understandable to them.

For example, suppose you want your students to develop a collage about <u>Inventions of the 20th Century</u>. When you brainstorm criteria for assessing this product, your list might look something like this:

Collage of 20th Century Inventions

1. Accuracy	6. Creative *
2. Has a solid backing *	7. Correct for time period
3. Neatness *	8. Shows relationships between inventions
4. Number of inventions shown	9. Title *
5. Pictures overlap *	10. Labels *

From this list, you can pick which of the criteria are relevant to **any** collage (indicated by *) and which are targeting the content of <u>Inventions of the 20th Century</u>. With this information, you can easily combine one or two items and create a Collage criteria card as follows:

Collage

1. Has a solid backing
2. Visually attractive and neat
3. Pictures overlap
4. Creative and original
5. Title and labels spelled correctly

Your assessment criteria for this product might then be:

1. Follows Collage criteria card

2. Accurate for time period

3. Has 10 or more inventions

4. Shows relationships between inventions

Like the indicator saying "Follows Collage criteria card," in this book you will see criteria that say: "Follows Model criteria card" or "Follows Map criteria card," etc. This is just a shorter way of saying to the student: *"I want your product to follow the criteria we have set for the product you are doing."* Using this method, you can indicate expectations for a superior product and at the same time emphasize the criteria related to the content and the standards.

On the next three pages are Product Criteria Cards for a wide variety of products. They are all products and performances that are found in the student activities in this book. Refer to them when the assessment criteria indicates a Criteria Card. Copy them for your students as needed.

Because you may assign products not included on these pages, use the blank form on page 24 to write your own Criteria Cards or use the customizable form on *Activities and Assessments* CD.

Product Criteria Cards

Brochure

1. Pictures relate to topic
2. Attractive and neat layout
3. Folded with information on each panel
4. Neat and clear writing highlighting important points
5. Correct spelling

Concept Map/Web

1. Has major topic in center
2. Shows details about the topic with lines and/or circles radiating from the center
3. Visually shows relationships of details or ideas to one another
4. Neat and legible

Cartoon

1. Conveys a message
2. Clear writing with correct spelling
3. Neatly drawn
4. Humorous
5. Creative and original

Crossword Puzzle

1. Each word intersects with another in at least one space
2. Correct spelling
3. Accurate definitions indicating across and down
4. Neatly and clearly done

Chart

1. Well-organized sections divided by lines
2. Clear and neat writing
3. Has a title and sub-titles
4. Accurate information
5. Correct spelling

Diorama

1. Realistic depiction of scene
2. Sides have background scenery
3. 3-dimensional figures/objects in fore-ground
4. Durable construction
5. Accurate

Collage

1. Has a solid backing
2. Visually attractive and neat
3. Pictures overlap
4. Creative and original
5. Has title/labels spelled correctly

Drawing

1. Pictures are clear and understandable
2. Neatly done
3. Shows topic accurately

Comic Book/Comic Strip

1. Frames in correct sequence
2. Tells story or idea through pictures
3. Characters/objects clearly drawn
4. Clear writing with correct spelling
5. Humor
6. Original and creative

Flowchart or Diagram

1. Has items in sequential order
2. Shows relationship between items by use of arrows or lines
3. Labels and items are neatly written
4. Short explanation of each item

Product Criteria Cards

Game

1. Clear and understandable rules
2. Well constructed
3. Visually appealing
4. Relates to topic being studied

Model

1. Accurate representation
2. Durable and well-constructed
3. Neatness
4. Creative use of materials

Graph

1. Labels/Title
2. Accurate data plotted correctly
3. Ruled measurements
4. Easy to understand
5. Neatness

Mosaic

1. Picture or design clearly shown
2. Uses small bits of paper, glass, tile or other materials to make picture
3. Neatness
4. Has a solid backing

Illustrated Booklet

1. Has words that explain pictures
2. Pictures match topic
3. Organized in a logical fashion
4. Neat and visually appealing
5. Correct spelling and grammar

Mural

1. Hangs on a wall
2. Is a rectangular shape at least 12"x36"
3. Shows several objects, people, and/or scenes
4. Colorful and neat

Map

1. Correct location of places
2. Clearly written key and symbols
3. Has scale and compass rose
4. Labels/places spelled correctly
5. Shapes of places and distances are accurate
6. Neatness

Oral Report/Presentation

1. Voice projection, clarity and expression
2. Eye contact
3. Appropriate body language and gestures
4. Correct timing

Mobile

1. Items are balanced and hang from a central point or structure
2. Durable construction
3. Visually appealing
4. Creative
5. Relevant to topic

Picture Postcard

1. Picture in color on front of card
2. Picture is clear and understandable
3. Size 4"x5" or 4"x6"
4. Message included on back

Product Criteria Cards

Poem

1. Appropriate format and poetic structure
2. Title
3. Rich vocabulary
4. Relevant to subject
5. Correct spelling, mechanics and punctuation

Song

1. Appropriate content
2. Has a rhythm
3. Words and music go together
4. Can be sung; auditory appeal

Poster

1. Title correctly spelled
2. Attractive/colorful visuals
3. Clear and neat writing
4. Original and creative
5. Shows topic well

Tableau

1. Scene is accurate and conveys information about topic
2. Costumes are accurate for person and time period
3. No movement or talking during viewing
4. Stays in character

PowerPoint Presentation

1. Visually appealing
2. Pictures and words are coordinated
3. Organization
4. Incorporates technological options that are available
5. Technology works appropriately

Time Line

1. Title
2. Chronological order
3. Important events indicated
4. Well-plotted time spans
5. Neat and legible
6. Correct spelling

Radio Report

1. Clear and understandable
2. Uses descriptive words
3. Recording quality is good
4. Has sound effects or music
5. Stays within time limits

Venn Diagram

1. Has two or more overlapping circles
2. Legible and neat
3. Shows similarities and differences
4. Has title and conclusions

Script for Skit or Play

1. Dialog for all characters clearly indicated
2. Stage directions included
3. Correct spelling, grammar and punctuation
4. Organized and interesting
5. Neatly written or typed

Video

1. Filming is clear
2. Organized flow of events
3. Accurate timing
4. Voice, music and/or sound effects are clear and understandable

Product Criteria Cards

_____

1.
2.
3.
4.
5.

_____

1.
2.
3.
4.
5.

_____

1.
2.
3.
4.
5.

_____

1.
2.
3.
4.
5.

_____

1.
2.
3.
4.
5.

_____

1.
2.
3.
4.
5.

_____

1.
2.
3.
4.
5.

_____

1.
2.
3.
4.
5.

_____

1.
2.
3.
4.
5.

_____

1.
2.
3.
4.
5.

Tic-Tac-Toe Student Choice Activities

One of the easiest ways to organize student choice activities is to use the Tic-Tac-Toe format. It is easy because both you and your students already know how the choices work. Students simply choose three activities going across, going down or going diagonally.

This format works well because it gives students choices and gives the teacher some control of the activities that students choose. If you give students a list of nine choices and ask them to choose three, many students will choose the three easiest, or the three requiring the least amount of work, or the three requiring no writing. In the Tic-Tac-Toe format, you can be sure that any set of choices will include a variety of types of activities. You can also make sure that no matter which configuration students choose, they will be completing activities that address the standards.

This section contains 24 Tic-Tac-Toe grids with 9 activities in each grid. The activities in these Tic-Tac-Toes are categorized in various ways such as by Learning Modalities, Bloom's Taxonomy, Multiple Intelligences or subject area. You will also find a corresponding page for each of the 24 grids, also written in the Tic-Tac-Toe format, with assessment indicators for each of the nine student choices.

The Tic-Tac-Toe activity grids in this book are appropriate for different grade levels. A few of them target primary students. The rest are appropriate for grades 3-5, 6-8 or 9-12. Look at your standards first to see if the student activities correlate to the standards. Then check to make sure they are at the appropriate level of difficulty for your students.

You will find the following Tic-Tac-Toe grids with corresponding assessments in this section:

How to Use the Tic-Tac-Toe Grids with Your Students

When using Tic-Tac-Toes, teachers typically give a copy to each student who will be doing the activities. Sometimes every student in the class will have a Tic-Tac-Toe. At other times these may be used for enrichment and extension activities for higher ability students or for review and practice for slower students. Students can work on the activities when they finish their other work or as an alternate activity instead of doing the grade level work.

In order for you to know which activities each student will be doing, record the numbers of the choices each student makes. Use the blank form on page 27 or the customizable form on the CD.

It is almost always good to assign a due date to students working on Tic-Tac-Toe activities. This helps them organize their time and their work, lessens the amount of wasted time, and encourages procrastinators to begin the task at hand. Sometimes you might ask students to put their work in portfolios or folders until all three activities are completed. At other times designate a place in the classroom where students can put completed work.

Involvement in Tic-Tac-Toe activities encourages and teaches independent learning. However, some students need more help than others. Have students keep a daily or weekly log of their progress when working on these activities. If necessary, decide on checkpoint dates when you can check each student's work and offer assistance if needed.

Assessing and Grading Tic-Tac-Toe Activities

For most students, getting a grade is an important part of doing their schoolwork. While a grade is not always necessary for Tic-Tac-Toe activities, usually you will want to assess them in some way. Each of the Tic-Tac-Toe activity grids in this book has a corresponding assessment grid. When you give the Tic-Tac-Toe activities to the students, duplicate the assessment indicators on the other side of the paper. This way, students will have both the activities and the assessments on one sheet of paper. The assessment indicators provide clear guidelines and criteria for students to follow when doing the activity.

There are no suggestions for the number of points each activity or each assessment indicator should be worth. The number of points for each activity and how you will score them is your decision. You can put the scores directly on the assessment portion of the Tic-Tac-Toe

when you return them to the students.

Many of the assessments in this book include a Suggested Extension. These are for students who can go above and beyond the assigned task or for those who can delve deeper into the topic. Extensions are usually not required, and students may think of other extensions they would like to do. You can include points for the extensions or can indicate their worth in some other way. Extensions are a good way to differentiate the activities for gifted and high-ability students.

Start with one of the Tic-Tac-Toes included in this book. After you have tried it, you may want to write some of your own. Use the form on page 77 to create the activities and the form on page 78 to design the corresponding assessments or use the customizable forms on the *Activities and Assessments* CD.

Student Activity Chart

Students' Names	1	2	3	4	5	6	7	8	9

1. Find out the current population of 5 African countries. Write this at the top of your paper. Then write and solve 5 math **word problems** using this information.	2. Make a **model** of something from traditional African culture such as a village, fighting instrument, headdress, etc. Make sure it is authentic for African culture.	3. Create **Jeopardy questions** about Africa. Include 5 categories of questions with 5 questions in each category. Write your questions and answers on index cards.
4. Make a **picture dictionary** of 20 African animals.	5. Research the history of 1 African country. Choose 5 significant events and write about each on a separate page. Write your conclusions about the country on page 6 of this 6-page **written report**.	6. Draw a current **map** of Africa. Names and boundaries of countries can change quickly, so make sure you have the most up-to-date information. Label all countries, capitals, and bodies of water.
7. Write a **journal** pretending you are an African living in the 1700s who has just been put on a slave ship to the new world. Describe your life in Africa and your feelings about what has happened to you.	8. Create a **brochure** advertising to tourists a country in Africa.	9. Use a **chart** to compare and contrast a country of your choice from northern Africa and a country of your choice from southern Africa. Include religion, shelter, clothing, foods, government and one other category of your choice.

I/we chose activities # _____, # _____, and # _____.

Name _____ **Date** _____ **Due date** _____

1. Math Word Problems Has population of 5 African countries ____ Word problems understandable and relate to population ____ Accurate information ____ Correct calculations ____ *Suggested extension: Give problems to classmates ____* Possible points = _____	**2. Model** Follows Model criteria card ____ Is authentic for culture ____ Shows an understanding of African life ____ Creativity ____ *Suggested extension: Research what this object was used for and report to the class ____* Possible points = _____	**3. Jeopardy Questions** Has 25 questions ____ Questions are in 5 categories ____ Accurate information ____ Neatly written ____ *Suggested extension: Organize a Jeopardy game for 3 classmates using your questions* Possible points = _____
4. Picture Dictionary Has 20 African animals ____ Each animal is illustrated ____ Correct definitions ____ Alphabetical order ____ *Suggested extension: Include more than 20 African animals including little known animals ____* Possible points = _____	**5. Written Report** Includes 5 events with 1 explained per page ____ Conclusions relate to information about the events ____ Correct grammar, spelling and punctuation ____ *Suggested extension: Create maps or illustrations ____* Possible points = _____	**6. Map** Follows Map criteria card ____ Accurate with current information ____ All countries, capitals and bodies of water accurately labeled and correctly placed ____ *Suggested extension: Explain why the map of Africa changes so often ____* Possible points = _____
7. Journal Correct spelling, punctuation and grammar ____ Point of view is clear ____ Accurate information ____ Historically correct details ____ *Suggested extension: Write another journal from the point of view of the Captain of the ship ____* Possible points = _____	**8. Brochure** Follows Brochure criteria card ____ Highlights important cities and tourist attractions ____ Includes a map ____ Uses persuasive language ____ *Suggested extension: Figure out the cost of visiting these places ____* Possible points = _____	**9. Chart** Follows Chart criteria card ____ Includes 6 categories ____ Has 1 country from north Africa and 1 from south Africa ____ At least 3 resources used ____ *Suggested extension: Write your conclusions in a paragraph ____* Possible points = _____

Points for activities: #_____ = _____ pts., #_____ = _____ pts., #_____ = _____ pts.

Name _____ Total points _____ Grade _____

1. Make a **concept map or web** showing important facts and ideas about Buddhism. *(Knowledge)*	**2.** Make 4 **picture postcards** showing something from each of the following places: China, Japan, North Korea, and South Korea. Write a message on the back of each postcard telling about the picture. *(Comprehension)*	**3.** **Plan a trip** to 5 Chinese cities. Mark each of the cities on a map and highlight your route. Calculate the distances between each city. *(Application)*
4. Make a **set of graphs** comparing North and South Korea. Write conclusions based on the information from your graphs. *(Analysis)*	**5.** Write a **haiku** describing life in Japan or China during the Japanese feudal period or the time of the Chinese dynasties. *(Synthesis)*	**6.** Write a 2-page **paper** giving your opinion about the relationship between China and Taiwan and their relationship to the United States. Give reasons to back up your opinions. *(Evaluation)*
7. Find out about the Japanese education system. Compare and contrast it to American education. Write an **editorial** telling which system you think is best and why. *(Evaluation)*	**8.** Create a **trifold brochure** advertising Japan, China, and South Korea as tourist destinations. Use each folded section of the inside of the brochure for a separate country with the outside featuring the region as a whole. *(Application)*	**9.** Make a **Venn diagram** comparing and contrasting Shintoism and Confucianism. *(Analysis)*

I/we chose activities # _____, #_____, and #_____.

Name _____ **Date** _____ **Due date** _____

1. Concept Map or Web	**2. Picture Postcards**	**3. Trip Planning**
Follows Concept Map criteria card _____	Follows Picture Postcard criteria card _____	5 Chinese cities marked _____
Has at least 10 facts about Buddhism _____	Message matches picture _____	Route between cities highlighted _____
Accurate information _____	Picture is about the country _____	Accurate calculations _____
Shows interrelationships of facts and ideas _____	Correct information _____	Neatness _____
	Has one postcard for each country _____	*Suggested extension: Write a story about your trip including what you did and what you saw* _____
Possible points = _____	Possible points = _____	Possible points = _____

4. Set of Graphs	**5. Haiku**	**6. Opinion Paper**
At least 3 separate sets of information are graphed _____	Written in correct haiku form __	Accurate facts _____
Follows Graph criteria card _____	Accurate information ___	Opinion is clear _____
Accurate data on graphs _____	Includes historic details about this time period _____	Reasons for opinion are stated and examples given _____
Conclusions are logical _____	Correct spelling _____	Correct spelling, punctuation and grammar _____
Conclusions are written in paragraph form _____	*Suggested extension: Decorate with Asian style illustration* _____	*Suggested extension: Include data, graphs and charts* _____
Possible points = _____	Possible points = _____	Possible points = _____

7. Editorial	**8. Brochure**	**9. Venn Diagram**
Correct spelling, punctuation and grammar _____	Follows Brochure criteria card _____	Follows Venn Diagram criteria card _____
Point of view is clear _____	Highlights important details, cities and tourist attractions _____	Accurate information _____
Accurate information _____	Inside section is divided into thirds with 1 section for each country _____	Similarities and differences clearly shown _____
Includes details and examples _____	Outside of brochure includes entire region _____	At least 3 resources used _____
Suggested extension: Include China and Korea in addition to Japan _____		
Possible points = _____	Possible points = _____	Possible points = _____

Points for activities: #_____ = _____ pts., #_____ = _____ pts., #_____ = _____ pts.

Name _____ **Total points** _____ **Grade** _____

1. Find out about the history and significance of Anzac Day and how the people of Australia celebrate it. Pretend you are an American reporter in Australia on Anzac Day. Tape a 5-minute **radio report** telling Americans about it.	**2.** Make a **boomerang**, and decorate it with Aboriginal-style artwork.	**3.** Create **Jeopardy questions** about Australia. Include 5 categories of questions with 5 questions in each category. Write your questions and answers on index cards.
4. Make a **picture dictionary** of 20 Australian animals.	**5.** Write a **myth or legend** telling how the Southern Cross constellation was formed. Find out what the Southern Cross is and what it looks like before you begin.	**6.** Draw a **world map** with Australia at the top and the Pacific Ocean in the middle. Label all directions, continents, and oceans.
7. Write a **journal** pretending you are a convict on the First Fleet to Australia. Do research about the convicts coming to Australia in 1788 so your account is accurate and detailed.	**8.** Create a **brochure** advertising Australia to tourists.	**9.** Listen to the song *"Waltzing Matilda."* Find out what the song is about and make a **diorama** showing the scene in the song.

I/we chose activities # _____, #_____, and #_____.

Name _____ **Date** _____ **Due date**_____

1. Radio Report	2. Boomerang	3. Jeopardy questions
Shows understanding of Anzac Day history ____ Includes celebration details ____ Accurate information ____ Follows Radio Report criteria card ____ *Suggested extension: Include interview or typical music ____* Possible points = _____	Correct shape ____ Has Aboriginal artwork ____ Neatness ____ Creativity ____ *Suggested extension: Research what boomerangs were used for and report to the class ____* Possible points = _____	Has 25 questions ____ Questions are in 5 categories ____ Accurate information ____ Neatly written ____ *Suggested extension: Organize a Jeopardy game for 3 classmates using your questions* Possible points = _____
4. Picture Dictionary	5. Myth or Legend	6. World Map
Has 20 Australian animals ____ Each animal is illustrated ____ Correct definitions ____ Alphabetical order ____ *Suggested extension: Include more than 20 Australian animals including little known animals ____* Possible points = _____	Has a beginning, middle and end ____ Relates to the Southern Cross ____ Interesting and creative ____ Correct grammar, spelling and punctuation ____ *Suggested extension: Include other constellations ___* Possible points = _____	Follows Map criteria card ____ Australia is at the top and in the middle ____ Correct directions (N/S/E/W) ____ Continents and oceans accurately labeled and correctly placed ____ *Suggested extension: Explain why this would be a normal perspective for Australians ____* Possible points = _____
7. Journal	8. Brochure	9. Diorama
Correct spelling, punctuation and grammar ____ Point of view is clear ____ Accurate information ____ Historically correct details ____ *Suggested extension: Write another journal from the point of view of the Captain of the ship ____* Possible points = _____	Follows Brochure criteria card ____ Highlights important cities and tourist attractions ____ Includes a map ____ Uses persuasive language ____ *Suggested extension: Figure out the cost of visiting these places ____* Possible points = _____	Follows Diorama criteria card ____ Scene is accurate for song ____ Words of the song shown in diorama are displayed ____ At least 3 resources used ____ *Suggested extension: Play or sing the song for your class ____* Possible points = _____

Points for activities: #_____ = _____ pts.,   #_____ = _____ pts.,   #_____ = _____ pts.

Name _____   Total points _____   Grade _____

1. Create a **character map or web** for your favorite character in the story. Show both character traits and events.	**2.** Produce a 3-minute **video news report** about an incident in the story involving 1 or more characters.	**3.** Decide on 5 or more criteria by which to judge characters. Design a **report card** using these criteria, and make a separate report card for at least 3 characters. Include grades and a comment section for each where you write specific comments about the character.
4. Create a **Dialog Book Jacket** where you write a description of 1 character on the left hand flap of the book jacket and another character on the right hand flap. Write a dialog between the 2 characters inside the middle panel. Illustrate your book jacket on the outside of the middle panel.	**5.** Do a **geometric character analysis** of several characters. Select 1 geometric shape to represent each character. Place each shape on a piece of paper so that you show their relationships with one another. Explain your shapes, color, size, placement, and connecting lines by referring to specific details in the story.	**6.** Dress like your favorite character and **role play** an important part of the story.
7. Draw a **Venn Diagram** to compare and contrast 2 characters in the story.	**8.** Write an **epilogue** to the story that tells what happened to 1 character after the story is over.	**9.** Write a **letter** to a character in the story telling how his or her life is like yours OR how it is very different from yours.

I/we chose activities # _____, #_____, and #_____.

Name _____ **Date** _____ **Due date** _____

1. Map or Web	2. Video News Report	3. Character Report Card
Shows at least 5 character traits ____ Includes at least 5 events ____ Shows how character acted in these events ____ Neat and readable visual ____ *Suggested extensions: Show illustrations included on map; Show interrelationships between characters* ____	Follows Video criteria card ____ Clearly explains incident ____ Accurate description of character's actions ____ Well organized report ____ *Suggested extension: Compare to other incidents in this story or with other stories* ____	5 criteria listed ____ Has report cards for 3 characters ____ Comments show knowledge about characters ____ *Suggested extensions: Include more than 3 characters; develop report card for self based on same criteria* ____
Possible points = _____	Possible points = _____	Possible points = _____
4. Dialog Book Jacket	**5. Geometric Character Analysis**	**6. Role Play**
Has written description of 2 characters ____ Realistic dialogue ____ Relevant illustration ____ Correct spelling, mechanics, and grammar ____ *Suggested extension: Create 2 dialogs in 2 different settings* ____	Shapes, sizes, etc. reflect different characters ____ Clearly explains visual in writing or orally ____ Explanation shows relationships between characters and plot ____ Visually attractive and neat ____	Accurate costume for character ____ Role play dramatizes story correctly ____ Follows Skit criteria card ____ *Suggested extension: Use 2 or more characters* ____
Possible points = _____	Possible points = _____	Possible points = _____
7. Venn Diagram	**8. Epilogue**	**9. Letter**
Character traits of each are clear and accurate ____ Similarities and differences plainly seen in diagram ____ Conclusions stated in sentence form ____ Neat and legible ____ *Suggested extension: Design a Venn diagram showing 3 characters* ____	Has at least 3 paragraphs ____ Correct grammar, mechanics and spelling ____ Well organized ____ Consistent character traits when compared with story ____ *Suggested extension: Make writing style similar to author* ____	Explanation is clear in showing your life and the character's ____ Has details and examples to illustrate points ____ Correct mechanics, spelling and grammar ____ Follows correct form for letter ____
Possible points = _____	Possible points = _____	Possible points = _____

Points for activities: #_____ = _____ pts.,   #_____ = _____ pts.,   #_____ = _____ pts.

Name _____ **Total points** _____ **Grade** _____

Book Report
Tic-Tac-Toe for Student Choice Activities

1. Choose 2 characters from your book. With another person, **role play** a scene from the book featuring these 2 characters. *(Bodily/Kinesthetic)*	2. Write a **different ending to your story**. This should change what happened in the last chapter of the book. *(Verbal/Linguistic)*	3. Draw at least 3 **comic strips** that highlight 3 important events in your book. Make sure the dialogue is realistic for the characters. *(Visual/Spatial)*
4. Design a **poster** advertising your book. Include interesting details about the book that would make others want to read it. *(Visual/Spatial)*	5. Create **song lyrics and music** to tell about your book. Use the book title as the song title. Perform for your class or record your song on audio tape. *(Musical/Rhythmic)*	6. Draw a **picture** and write a **paragraph** describing the outdoor setting (or settings) of your book. How did the setting affect the story? *(Naturalist)*
7. Write a **letter** to the author telling why you liked the book or why you didn't like it. Give valid reasons for your opinion. *(Intrapersonal)*	8. Make an **information cube** about your book with the following on the 6 different sides of the cube: title characters setting plot favorite part illustration of scene *(Verbal/Linguistic Bodily/Kinesthetic)*	9. Make a **time line** sequencing 10 important events that happened in the book. *(Logical/Mathematical)*

I/we chose activities # _____, # _____, and # _____.

Name _____ **Date** _____ **Due date** _____

1. Role Play	**2. Alternate Ending**	**3. Comic Strips**
Costumes and props realistic for characters _____	Appropriate for characters and setting _____	Follows Comic Strip criteria card _____
Accurate scene _____	Ending creative and feasible _____	Each comic strip has 4 or more panels _____
Good voice projection and expression _____	Correct spelling, punctuation and grammar _____	Events accurately portrayed _____
Has written script _____	At least two pages _____	Realistic dialogue _____
Possible points = _____	Possible points = _____	Possible points = _____
4. Poster	**5. Song Lyrics & Music**	**6. Picture & Paragraph**
Follows Poster criteria card _____	Follows Song criteria card _____	Picture and paragraph show natural setting _____
Includes several details about the book _____	Lyrics include several important details about book _____	Has written and visual details of setting(s) _____
Uses persuasive language _____	Performance is clear and musically pleasing _____	Explains ways the setting affected the story _____
		Correct mechanics, spelling and grammar _____
Possible points = _____	Possible points = _____	Possible points = _____
7. Letter	**8. Information Cube**	**9. Time Line**
Likes or dislikes clearly stated _____	Cube is sturdy and has 6 sides _____	Follows Time Line criteria card _____
3 or more reasons given to support point of view _____	Has needed information and details on each side _____	Has 10 or more events _____
Reasons supported by facts or examples _____	Accurate for book read _____	Correct sequencing of events following story in book _____
Correct spelling, punctuation and grammar _____	Neat, legible and visually attractive _____	
Possible points = _____	Possible points = _____	Possible points = _____

Points for activities: #_____ = _____ pts., #_____ = _____ pts., #_____ = _____ pts.

Name _____ **Total points** _____ **Grade** _____

1. Research common diseases in the new world during the 1700s. Make a **chart** listing 5 diseases, medicines, and treatments used and the mortality rate for early settlers.	**2.** Write an **illustrated story** about a voyage to the new world.	**3.** Design an **advertising flyer or poster** to convince people to make the voyage to the new world. Include reasons for going, transportation for getting there, and information about settlements.
4. Make a **speech** convincing your classmates NOT to travel and settle in the new world. Include real dangers and myths people may have believed at the time.	**5.** Draw a **map** of the new world in 1750. Label colonies and other land areas in North America.	**6.** Research information about the first Thanksgiving. Make a **Truth and Fiction** chart with 2 columns. List beliefs about the first Thanksgiving that are true in one column and ones that are false or that we're not sure about in the other.
7. Write a **diary entry** about the arrival of a group of settlers from the point of view of an Indian.	**8.** Find a **recipe** for a typical food eaten during the 1700s. Prepare it, and serve it to the class. Include the recipe and information about it.	**9.** Construct **puppets**, and put on a **puppet show** about the arrival of a group of new settlers to the new world. Perform this with at least 1 other person.

I/we chose activities # _____, #_____, and #_____.

Name _____ Date _____ Due date _____

1. Chart	2. Illustrated Story	3. Flyer or Poster
Follows Chart criteria card _____ Lists 5 common diseases of the 1700s _____ Has accurate facts and details about medicines/treatments and mortality rates _____ *Suggested extension: Show how these same diseases are treated today* _____ Possible points = _____	Has a beginning, middle, and end _____ Includes factual details about voyages to the new world _____ Illustrations relate to story _____ Correct mechanics, spelling and grammar _____ *Suggested extension: Design a map showing route* _____ Possible points = _____	Follows Poster criteria card _____ Has accurate facts and details about transportation and settlements _____ Uses persuasive language in giving reasons for going _____ *Suggested extension: Include examples of real settlers with accurate historical details* _____ Possible points = _____
4. Persuasive Speech	5. Map	6. Truth and Fiction Chart
Follows Oral Presentation criteria card _____ Includes 3 real dangers with examples _____ Includes 3 myths people believed at the time _____ Uses persuasive language _____ *Suggested extension: Include visuals in presentation* _____ Possible points = _____	Follows Map criteria card _____ Accurate _____ Colonies and other land in North America correctly labeled _____ *Suggested extension: Include little known details such as Indian tribal lands and important waterways* ____ Possible points = _____	Follows Chart criteria card _____ Historically accurate _____ Resources listed _____ Categorized correctly _____ *Suggested extension: Write a short essay explaining the reasons for these different beliefs* _____ Possible points = _____
7. Diary Entry	8. Recipe & Food	9. Puppets & Show
Written from Indian point of view _____ Setting described well _____ Describes actions of new settlers _____ Correct mechanics, spelling and grammar _____ *Suggested extension: Create illustrations showing arrival* _____ Possible points = _____	Food is typical for time period _____ Prepared food follows recipe _____ Includes written recipe and information about it _____ *Suggested extension: Create a small cookbook containing recipes from the 1700s* _____ Possible points = _____	Puppets historically accurate and detailed _____ Has a written script _____ Historically correct details about arrival to the new world _____ Voices are clear and loud _____ *Suggested extension: Perform for other classes* _____ Possible points = _____

Points for activities: #_____ = _____ pts., #_____ = _____ pts., #_____ = _____ pts.

Name _____ **Total points** _____ **Grade** _____

1. Make a **Venn diagram** comparing Western Europe and Eastern Europe. What conclusions can you make?	**2.** Make a **model** of any famous European landmark such as the Eiffel Tower, Leaning Tower of Pisa, or Stonehenge. Include a written display card explaining why it is important.	**3.** Create **Jeopardy questions** about Europe. Include 5 categories of questions with 5 questions in each category. Write your questions and answers on index cards.
4. Choose 1 European country. Make a **time line** of 20 important events in its history.	**5.** Find out what the euro is worth compared to the U.S. dollar. Rewrite ten **newspaper ads** from an American newspaper using euros instead of dollars.	**6.** Make a **pro and con chart** listing at least 5 advantages and 5 disadvantages of Europe becoming 1 country. Write a conclusion explaining your opinion for or against becoming 1 country and why you feel this way.
7. Write a **journal** pretending you are living for 2 weeks in a European country of your choice. Make sure your account is realistic, accurate, and detailed for the country you have chosen.	**8.** Create a **brochure** advertising Europe to tourists.	**9.** Research wars that have involved both the United States and Europe. Make a **diorama** showing a scene from 1 of these wars.

I/we chose activities # _____, #_____, and #_____.

Name _____ Date _____ Due date _____

Assessment
Europe Tic-Tac-Toe

1. Venn Diagram Follows Venn Diagram criteria card ____ Similarities and differences clearly shown ____ Accurate information ____ Logical conclusions ____ *Suggested extension: Compare 2 eastern European or 2 western European countries* ____ Possible points = _____	**2. Model of Landmark** Follows Model criteria card ____ Has information about the landmark on a display card ____ Neatness ____ Correct spelling on card ____ *Suggested extension: Research the history of this place and report to the class* ____ Possible points = _____	**3. Jeopardy questions** Has 25 questions ____ Questions are in 5 categories ____ Accurate information ____ Neatly written ____ *Suggested extension: Organize a Jeopardy game for 3 classmates using your questions* Possible points = _____
4. Time Line Follows Time Line criteria card ____ Has 20 important events ____ Events are about 1 European country ____ Accurate information ____ *Suggested extension: Illustrate time line* ____ Possible points = _____	**5. Newspaper Ads** Accurate information ____ Correct computations ____ Has ten newspaper ads rewritten in euros ____ Correct spelling ____ Neatness ____ Possible points = _____	**6. Pro and Con Chart** Follows Chart criteria card ____ Lists 5 advantages and 5 disadvantages ____ Logical conclusion explaining reasons ____ Correct grammar, spelling and mechanics ____ Possible points = _____
7. Journal Correct spelling, punctuation and grammar ____ Has an entry for each day for 2 weeks ____ Accurate information ____ Correct details for country ____ *Suggested extension: Include map or illustrations* ____ Possible points = _____	**8. Brochure** Follows Brochure criteria card ____ Highlights important cities and tourist attractions ____ Includes a map ____ Uses persuasive language ____ *Suggested extension: Figure out the cost of visiting these places* ____ Possible points = _____	**9. Diorama** Follows Diorama criteria card ____ Scene is historically accurate ____ Has label with name of battle or event and date ____ At least 3 resources used ____ *Suggested extension: Do a short oral report for your class about this battle, event or the war it was part of* ____ Possible points = _____

Points for activities: #_____ = _____ pts., #_____ = _____ pts., #_____ = _____ pts.

Name _____ **Total points** _____ **Grade** _____

Famous Artists
Tic-Tac-Toe for Student Choice Activities

1.
 	
Create a **time line** showing important events in the lives of 10 different artists.
 	
(Visual)
	2.
	
	Choose a famous artist and give an **oral report** telling about his or her:
	
	   • Early life
	   • Friends
	   • Style or technique
	   • Major problems
	   • Most famous work
	
	(Verbal)
		3.
		
		Find a good website that tells about artists of a certain period and shows examples of their work. Print **5 examples and write a sentence about each**. Be sure to reference the website.
		
		(Technological)

4. Make a 3-minute **video** of a scene or event in the life of an artist of your choice. *(Technological)*	**5.** Create a **3-D piece of art** in the style of the artist of your choice. *(Kinesthetic)*	**6.** Create an **Encyclopedia of Famous Artists**. It should include at least 20 artists. *(Verbal)*
7. Research the lives of 2 artists. Create a **Venn diagram** comparing and contrasting them. *(Visual/Verbal)*	**8.** Create a **poster** advertising a sale of artwork. Show prints from 5 famous artists on your poster. You can draw the poster or create it on the computer. *(All modalities)*	**9.** Draw or paint a **self-portrait** in the style of Picasso, Matisse or Van Gogh. *(Visual)*

I/we chose activities # _____, #_____, and #_____.

Name _____ Date _____ Due date _____

Assessment
Famous Artists Tic-Tac-Toe

1. Time Line Follows Time Line criteria card _____ Includes 10 artists _____ Accurate information _____ Events are important _____ *Suggested extension: Also show important world events on the time line* _____ Possible points = _____	**2. Oral Report** Follows Oral Report criteria card _____ Includes the 5 required items _____ Accurate information _____ *Suggested extension: Use visuals to go along with report* _____ Possible points = _____	**3. Website Examples** Website has examples of art from an historic period _____ Has 5 examples of artwork printed out _____ Has a sentence about each _____ Website accurately cited _____ *Suggested extension: Cite several websites and tell differences among them* _____ Possible points = _____
4. Video Follows Video criteria card _____ Scenery and props are historically accurate _____ Accurate information _____ Explains who the artist is _____ *Suggested extension: Use reproductions of artist's work in the video* _____ Possible points = _____	**5. 3-D Piece of Artwork** Durable construction _____ Has 3 dimensions _____ Artist's style is evident _____ Artist is indicated _____ *Suggested extension: Write a biography of the artist with pictures of artwork* _____ Possible points = _____	**6. Encyclopedia** Includes 20 artists _____ Has 1 or more paragraphs about each artist _____ Alphabetical order _____ Accurate information _____ *Suggested extensions: Include illustrations; include more than 20 artists* _____ Possible points = _____
7. Venn Diagram Follows Venn Diagram criteria card _____ Clearly shows similarities and differences _____ Accurate information _____ *Suggested extension: Make a Venn diagram with 3 circles and compare 3 artists* _____ Possible points = _____	**8. Poster** Follows Poster criteria card _____ Has prints from 5 artists _____ Artists names match prints _____ Written details about each print included on poster _____ *Suggested extension: Use persuasive language to encourage sales* _____ Possible points = _____	**9. Self Portrait** Done in the style of the artist _____ Can tell this is a portrait of you _____ Neat & colorful _____ *Suggested extension: Include print of artist's self-portrait and written comparison of the artist's self portrait and yours* _____ Possible points = _____

Points for activities: #_____ = _____ pts.,   #_____ = _____ pts.,   #_____ = _____ pts.

Name _____ **Total points** _____ **Grade** _____

1. Compile a list of factual questions for a region of the world. Design a **game** to play using these questions.	**2.** Make your **family tree** going back 3 or more generations. Identify the regions of the world each of your ancestors has come from. Write 2 important things about each person on your family tree.	**3.** Choose a continent. Gather information about population trends in 5 different countries on that continent. Generate a **graph** showing what you find.
4. Create a **poster** illustrating the Five Themes of Geography in the country or continent of your choice.	**5.** Make a **flow chart** showing how people in a community are interdependent.	**6.** Find out about the unique physical features in any geographical area of your choice. These might be mountains, rivers, canyons, lakes, caves, etc. Write a **myth** that explains how these features came to be.
7. Make a list of 20 things you find in a supermarket that are associated with any foreign country. Develop a 5-column **chart** showing: (1) how the items get to the supermarket (2) how many are purchased each year (3) cost of production (4) cost to purchase (5) other facts or information	**8.** **Interview** a person who is from or has lived in a foreign country for a number of years. Create interview questions that will help you find out about the history, population, culture, natural resources, etc. of the country. Write the interview questions and the answers you get.	**9.** Pretend that you are on a 21-day trip through the country or continent of your choice. Write a daily **travelogue** giving details about all that you see and do.

I/we chose activities # _____, # _____, and # _____.

Name _____ **Date** _____ **Due date** _____

1. Game Follows Game criteria card _____ Has at least 20 factual questions and answers _____ Accurate information _____ *Suggested extension: Play game with a classmate* _____ Possible points = _____	**2. Family Tree** Clear, neat visual _____ Regions for each ancestor clearly shown _____ Includes 2 important facts about each ancestor_____ Has 3 or more generations _____ *Suggested extension: Show locations of regions on a map* _____ Possible points = _____	**3. Graph** Follows Graph criteria card _____ Accurate information _____ Includes 5 or more countries from the same continent _____ *Suggested extension: Make 2 graphs showing population trends on 2 different continents. Write a paragraph explaining your conclusions* _____ Possible points = _____
4. Poster Follows Poster criteria card _____ All 5 themes included _____ Accurate illustration of each theme _____ Includes short written explanation of each theme _____ *Suggested extension: Create unique or creative pictures and iillustrations* _____ Possible points = _____	**5. Flow Chart** Follows Flow Chart criteria card ____ Various types of people in a community clearly shown _____ Roles of people defined _____ Includes at least 10 types of people _____ *Suggested extension: Take photos of people and include on Flow Chart* _____ Possible points = _____	**6. Myth** Follows Story criteria card _____ Includes explanation of how one or more physical features came to be _____ Creativity _____ Accurate for geographical location _____ *Suggested extension: Illustrate myth* _____ Possible points = _____
7. Chart Follows Chart criteria card _____ Has 5 columns with topics as assigned _____ Accurate information _____ Has 20 or more items _____ *Suggested extension: Write a 1-page paper stating your conclusions about trade with other countries* _____ Possible points = _____	**8. Interview** Questions are clear _____ Questions require more than yes and no answers _____ At least 10 questions _____ Questions and answers neatly written _____ *Suggested extension: Arrange for this person to speak to your class* ____ Possible points = _____	**9. Travelogue** Accurate details about places visited _____ All 21 days have a written entry ____ Correct grammar & spelling _____ At least 3 resources listed _____ *Suggested extension: Include illustrations and maps* _____ Possible points = _____

Points for activities: #_____ = _____ pts., #_____ = _____ pts., #_____ = _____ pts.

Name _____ **Total points** _____ **Grade** _____

1. Draw some type of **visual** that relates the 2 forms of cell division to the human life cycle.	**2.** Write a short **essay** explaining the problems and benefits that may result from genetic engineering.	**3.** **Search the Internet** for information about animals with genetic disorders. Print out what you find and summarize by developing your own **outline.**
4. Make a **time line** of genetically cloned animals. Start with the first known clone and continue to the present.	**5.** Choose 1 disease or condition that is caused by genetics or heredity. Write a **newspaper article** highlighting the most important things the general public needs to know about it.	**6.** Write a **short story** about the life of a gene on a chromosome.
7. Write a **report** about 3 different treatments for infertility. Include statistics and the pros and cons of each.	**8.** Design a **poster** that shows the process of the alternation of generations.	**9.** Make a **model** or models to show how genes and chromosomes work.

I/we chose activities # _____, # _____, and # _____.

Name _____ **Date** _____ **Due date** _____

1. Drawing/Visual	2. Essay	3. Internet Search & Outline
Visual clearly shows both forms _____ Accuracy of information _____ Relationship between the 2 forms is evident _____ Detailed and informational labels _____ Possible points = _____	Explanation clear and well organized _____ Problems and benefits identified _____ Balanced point of view_____ Writing mechanics, spelling and grammar are correct _____ Possible points = _____	Uses at least 5 Internet sites_____ Variety of information _____ Accurate summary highlighting important points _____ Follows correct outline form _____ Possible points = _____
4. Time Line	5. Newspaper Article	6. Short Story
Follows Time Line criteria card _____ Has at least 10 significant events _____ Details about each event included on time line _____ Both scientific and political events incorporated _____ Possible points = _____	Article is written in an interesting way so the public would like to read it _____ Accurate details about the disease or condition noted _____ Knowledge of genetics shown in explanation of the cause of disease or condition _____ Possible points = _____	Story has a beginning, middle and end _____ Story reflects knowledge of genes and chromosomes and their relationship to each other _____ Creativity_____ Correct spelling, grammar and mechanics _____ Possible points = _____
7. Written Report	8. Poster	9. Model(s)
3 treatments clearly stated _____ Statistics noted and shown in graph or chart form _____ Pros and cons plainly indicated _____ Correct spelling, mechanics and grammar _____ Possible points = _____	Follows Poster criteria card _____ Process clearly shown _____ Explanation of process included on poster _____ Possible points = _____	Follows Model criteria card _____ Accurately shows structure and form of genes and chromosomes _____ How they work is clearly seen from model(s) _____ Possible points = _____

Points for activities: #_____ = _____ pts., #_____ = _____ pts., #_____ = _____ pts.

Name _____ **Total points** _____ **Grade** _____

Geometry: 3-Dimensional Solids
Tic-Tac-Toe for Student Choice Activities

1.	2.	3.
Construct a Regular **Polyhedron** out of straws.	**List** the Seven Wonders of the World. Research and record the measurements of each. Using this information, find the surface area and volume of all Seven Wonders. Show all **information and calculations**.	**Interview** an architect and find out how he/she uses 3-dimensional figures in his/her designs. Write a **paper** summarizing what you learned.
4.	5.	6.
Create a **lesson plan** on Regular Polyhedrons and teach this lesson to the class.	Estimate the total surface area of your classroom. Then do the appropriate measurements and find the exact surface area. Compare the estimate to the exact area. Explain this process in **paragraph** form.	Make a **collage** of various polyhedrons. Label and give a definition of each polyhedron.
7.	8.	9.
Make a **model** of a new 3-dimensional solid that can be classified as a polyhedron and give it a name.	Make a **cube**. Place the digits 1 through 8 at the corners of the cube so that the sum of the four numbers for each face (side of the cube) is 18. Show your **calculations** on a separate piece of paper.	Make a **crossword puzzle** using at least 20 words that relate to 3-dimensional Solids.

I/we chose activities # _____, #_____, and #_____.

Name _____   Date _____ Due date _____

Assessment of Geometry: 3-Dimensional Solids Tic-Tac-Toe

1. Straw Polyhedron	2. List & Calculations	3. Interview & Paper
Follows Model criteria card _____ Name of polyhedron is labeled with basic information about it _____ Accurate shape for polyhedron selected _____ *Suggested extension: Make detailed drawing of faces, vertices and edges included with model* _____ Possible points = _____	Accurate list and measurements ___ Calculations mathematically correct _____ Process shown for solving each problem _____ *Suggested extension: Write 7 paragraphs telling other interesting facts about each Wonder* _____ Possible points = _____	Identifies architect _____ Accurate information about his/her work in the field _____ Explains architect's use of 3-dimensional figures _____ Correct grammar, spelling and punctuation _____ *Suggested extension: Include pictures of architect's designs* _____ Possible points = _____
4. Lesson Plan	**5. Paragraph**	**6. Collage**
Follows Oral Presentation criteria card _____ Correct information _____ Explains clearly – easy to understand _____ Answers questions well _____ *Suggested extension: Give test or quiz and grade it* _____ Possible points = _____	Shows difference in estimated and exact surface area _____ Accurate calculations _____ Process explained in detail _____ Correct grammar, spelling and punctuation _____ *Suggested extension: Do the same calculations in your house* _____ Possible points = _____	Follows Collage criteria card _____ Shows 5 or more different polyhedrons _____ Correct labels & definitions _____ *Suggested extension: Show architecture with several polyhedrons in 1 building* _____ Possible points = _____
7. Model	**8. Cube & Calculations**	**9. Crossword Puzzle**
Follows Model criteria card _____ Original creation and name for polyhedron _____ Has characteristics of a polyhedron _____ *Suggested extension: Create 2 new types of polyhedrons that can be used together. List possible uses* _____ Possible points = _____	Follows Model criteria card _____ Sum of all corners of the cube are mathematically correct _____ Calculations shown on paper _____ *Suggested extension: Do similar calculations done on a different polyhedron* _____ Possible points = _____	Follows Crossword Puzzle criteria card _____ Has at least 20 words related to polyhedrons _____ *Suggested extension: Make the shape of the puzzle reflect polyhedrons* _____ Possible points = _____

Points for activities: #_____ = _____ pts., #_____ = _____ pts., #_____ = _____ pts.

Name _____ **Total points** _____ **Grade** _____

1. Design a **symbol** for the Native American tribe of your choice. Make sure the symbol shows information and details about this tribe.	**2.** Write a **short story** about a boy or girl who traveled from North Carolina to Oklahoma on the Cherokee's "Trail of Tears".	**3.** On a **map** of North America, label the **location** of 10 important Native American tribes in the 1700s.
4. Make an **illustrated dictionary** of 20 important words related to Native Americans.	**5.** Make a **chart** comparing and contrasting Plains Indians and Pueblo Indians.	**6.** Construct a **diorama** showing a typical village or living area of the tribe of your choice.
7. Write a **diary entry** about a day in your life as if you were a Native American. Include information about your tribe and some typical customs or activities.	**8.** Make a **model** of a totem pole that represents your family.	**9.** Construct **puppets** and put on a **puppet show** about life in a Native American tribe. This should be done with at least 1 other person.

I/we chose activities # _____, #_____, and #_____.

Name _____ Date _____ Due date _____

© Pieces of Learning

Assessment
Native Americans Tic-Tac-Toe

1. Symbol Symbol is clear & colorful _____ Creativity _____ Shows accurate information about tribe _____ Tribe is labeled _____ *Suggested extension: Add written information about tribe* _____ Possible points = _____	**2. Short Story** Has a beginning, middle and end _____ Includes factual details about the "Trail of Tears" _____ Interesting characters _____ Correct mechanics, spelling and grammar _____ *Suggested extension: Include a map showing the route* _____ Possible points = _____	**3. Map Locations** Correct locations for each _____ Names of tribes spelled correctly _____ 10 or more tribes _____ Neat and legible _____ *Suggested extension: Write information about each tribe included on map* _____ Possible points = _____
4. Illustrated Dictionary Contains 20 words about Native Americans _____ Illustrations relate to words_____ Correct definitions _____ Alphabetical order _____ *Suggested extension: Include more than 20 words about a variety of tribes* _____ Possible points = _____	**5. Chart** Follows Chart criteria card _____ Has facts and details about both groups _____ Similarities and differences clearly shown _____ *Suggested extension: Make another chart comparing 2 types of Plains or 2 types of Pueblo Indians* _____ Possible points = _____	**6. Diorama** Follows Diorama criteria card _____ Historically accurate _____ Tribe clearly labeled _____ *Suggested extension: Include music, sound effects and/or other interesting additions* _____ Possible points = _____
7. Diary Entry Includes entire day _____ Setting described well _____ Includes customs/activities _____ Correct mechanics, spelling and grammar _____ *Suggested extension: Include creative dialog using Native American words* _____ Possible points = _____	**8. Totem Pole Model** Follows Model criteria card _____ Has several details or symbols representing family _____ Style is like a real totem pole _____ *Suggested extension: Explain symbols used on totem pole (include on separate sheet of paper)* _____ Possible points = _____	**9. Puppets & Show** Puppets historically accurate and detailed _____ Has a written script _____ Correct details about tribal life _____ Voices are clear and loud _____ *Suggested extension: Perform for other classes* _____ Possible points = _____

Points for activities: #_____ = _____ pts., #_____ = _____ pts., #_____ = _____ pts.

Name _____ **Total points** _____ **Grade** _____

1. **List** at least 20 things you could find in the grocery store that come from the ocean. Have a variety of items on your list.	**2.** Write 5 **safety tips** for playing in or near the ocean. Draw a **picture** illustrating each.	**3.** Make an ocean **collage** using different types of pictures and materials. Include written **facts** about oceans.
4. Design a **T-shirt** about oceans. Wear it and show it to the class.	**5.** Make a **word search** using at least 20 ocean words.	**6.** Read a **book** about oceans. Use a cassette recorder and tell someone about it on **tape**.
7. Write a **story** called "How the Swordfish Got Its Name".	**8.** Make an **illustrated booklet** of ocean plant life.	**9.** Draw a **map of the ocean floor**. Make a key for your map.

I/we chose activities # _____, #_____, and #_____.

Name _____ **Date** _____ **Due date** _____

1. List	2. Safety Tips & Pictures	3. Collage with Facts
List has 20 or more items that come from the ocean _____ Variety of different types of items included _____ *Suggested extension: Make a map of the world accurately labeled showing where each item came from* _____ Possible points = _____	Has 5 good and useful tips _____ Pictures relate to tips _____ *Suggested extension: Write a paragraph explaining why each tip is important to follow* _____ Possible points = _____	Follows Collage criteria card _____ Clearly shows some aspect of oceans _____ Facts included on collage or on back of paper _____ *Suggested extension: Create the collage so that it reflects your emotions about oceans and the 'feel' of oceans to the viewer* _____ Possible points = _____
4. T-Shirt	**5. Word Search**	**6. Book Tape**
Design shows knowledge about oceans _____ Plant and/or animal life included in design _____ Originality/creativity _____ Neatness _____ *Suggested extension: On the T-shirt write prose or poetry that has interesting or unique ideas about oceans* _____ Possible points = _____	All 20 words relate to oceans _____ Words spelled correctly _____ Neat & well organized _____ Includes an answer key _____ *Suggested extension: Define words on separate sheet of paper* _____ Possible points = _____	Book at appropriate reading level for student _____ 5 minutes on tape _____ Clear and understandable _____ Accurate summary of book _____ *Suggested extension: Include music, sound effects and/or other interesting additions* _____ Possible points = _____
7. Story	**8. Illustrated Booklet**	**9. Map of Ocean Floor**
Story has a beginning, middle and end _____ Creativity _____ Correct spelling, punctuation and mechanics _____ Story relates to title _____ *Suggested extension: Make factual knowledge of swordfish evident in story* _____ Possible points = _____	Follows Illustrated Booklet criteria card _____ At least 10 plants _____ Labels with facts about each plant _____ Well organized _____ *Suggested extension: Show clearly relationships between plants* _____ Possible points = _____	Follows Map criteria card _____ Key realistic & accurate _____ Shows typical ocean floor _____ Includes representative animal and plant life on ocean floor _____ *Suggested extension: Show 2 ocean floors from different climate regions. Make a chart comparing and contrasting them* _____ Possible points = _____

Points for activities: #_____ = _____ pts.,   #_____ = _____ pts.,   #_____ = _____ pts.

Name _____ **Total points** _____ **Grade** _____

1. Make a **board game** that can be played to learn at least 20 facts about the periodic table. *(Bodily/Kinesthetic)*	**2.** Write a **report** explaining how the periodic table is organized. *(Verbal/Linguistic)*	**3.** Make an **illustrated time line** showing the discovery dates of at least 20 elements on the periodic table. *(Visual/Spatial)*
4. Write 20 knowledgeable **questions** about the periodic table that you could use to interview a chemist. *(Interpersonal)*	**5.** Select 20 symbols on the periodic table. Include their names and something about each in a **song or rap** about them. Perform for the class or record on audio tape. *(Musical/Rhythmic)*	**6.** Create a **collage** that illustrates where various elements on the periodic table occur in nature. Label each element. *(Naturalist)*
7. Write a **letter** to Mr. Mendeleev telling him why you like or do not like his organization of the periodic table. Give at least 3 reasons to support your point of view. *(Intrapersonal)*	**8.** Design a **study guide** for students to use when studying the periodic table. It must have at least 20 questions or items. *(Verbal/Linguistic)*	**9.** Design a **graph** that shows the ratio or proportion of metal, metalloids and nonmetals that are on the periodic table. *(Mathematical/Logical)*

I/we chose activities # _____, #_____, and #_____.

Name _____   Date _____   Due date _____

© Pieces of Learning

1. Board Game	**2. Written Report**	**3. Illustrated Time Line**
Follows Game criteria card _____ Includes at least 20 facts _____ Facts are accurate and relate to periodic table _____ *Suggested extensions: Include more than 20 facts including little known or unusual facts; Make game unusual and challenging* _____ Possible points = _____	Clear explanation _____ Contains several examples to show organization of periodic table _____ Correct spelling, punctuation and grammar _____ Well organized report _____ *Suggested extension: Show problems with the table* _____ Possible points = _____	Follows Time Line criteria card _____ Discovery dates accurate_____ Illustrations relate to elements noted on time line _____ Has 20 elements _____ *Suggested extensions: Include more than 20 elements; include variety of types of elements* _____ Possible points = _____
4. Twenty Questions	**5. Song or Rap**	**6. Collage**
Has 20 questions _____ Questions show knowledge of periodic table_____ Answers to questions require more than 'yes' or 'no' _____ Questions are clear _____ *Suggested extension: Conduct the interview in person or via email and record the answers* _____ Possible points = _____	Follows Song criteria card _____ Includes 20 symbols _____ Accurate information about each element chosen _____ *Suggested extension: Teach the song to the class and have them sing it with you* _____ Possible points = _____	Follows Collage criteria card _____ Shows 20 elements _____ Accurate labels _____ *Suggested extension: Show how different elements interact in a natural setting* _____ Possible points = _____
7. Letter	**8. Study Guide**	**9. Graph**
Likes or dislikes clearly stated _____ 3 or more reasons to support point of view_____ Reasons supported by facts or examples _____ Correct spelling, punctuation and grammar_____ *Suggested extension: Show both viewpoints and reasons for each* _____ Possible points = _____	Guide has important information _____ Clear and accurate _____ Well organized _____ *Suggested extensions: Use creative or unique approach; use with a group of students to help them study* _____ Possible points = _____	Follows Graph criteria card _____ Accurate ratio and proportions shown _____ Includes lists of elements in categories _____ *Suggested extension: Show information on 2 or more different types of graphs* _____ Possible points = _____

Points for activities: #_____ = _____ pts., #_____ = _____ pts., #_____ = _____ pts.

Name _____ **Total points** _____ **Grade** _____

1.	2.	3.
Create a **board game** that teaches MLA rules for documenting sources.	Write a **report** explaining different style manuals and their origins. Give reasons why different subject areas use different styles.	Draw a series of **cartoons** that show different types of plagiarism. Include at least 3 different examples.
(Bodily/Kinesthetic)	*(Verbal/Linguistic)*	*(Visual/Spatial)*
4.	**5.**	**6.**
Contact an Internet provider of student essays or term papers. Ask 5 or more questions in an **email interview**. Present your findings in an **oral report** to the class.	Write a **song or rap** explaining how, why and what punctuation is used when documenting sources.	Create a **collage** showing various ways to document sources.
(Interpersonal)	*(Musical/Rhythmic)*	*(Visual/Spatial)*
7.	**8.**	**9.**
Write a **journal** from the point of view of a person who has been accused of plagiarism or breaking copyright laws. Include feelings, thoughts and decisions.	**Debate** with a classmate: All music should be completely free to copy and listen to in any format.	Make a **time line** showing changes in copyright laws.
(Intrapersonal)	*(Verbal/Linguistic)*	*(Logical/Mathematical)*

I/we chose activities # _____, #_____, and #_____.

Name _____ **Date** _____ **Due date** _____

Assessment
Plagiarism, Copyright and Documenting Sources Tic-Tac-Toe

1. Board game Follows Game criteria card ____ Includes 20 or more rules ____ Accurate information ____ *Suggested extension: Include ways to show how mistakes can be made and penalize game player when this happens ____* Possible points = _____	**2. Written Report** Includes 3 different style manuals ____ Explains origin of each style ___ Accurate information ____ Correct spelling, punctuation and grammar ____ *Suggested extension: Make charts or graphs to go along with report ____* Possible points = _____	**3. Cartoons** Follows Cartoon criteria card ___ Has 3 or more examples of plagiarism ____ Portrays realistic situations ____ *Suggested extension: Research legal implications and include this in your cartoons ____* Possible points = _____
4. Email Interview & Report Follows Oral Report criteria card ____ Has 5 or more questions ____ Questions include plagiarism and copyright issues ____ Accurate information ____ *Suggested extension: Include in report examples from Internet provider ____* Possible points = _____	**5. Song or Rap** Follows Song criteria card ___ Accurate information ____ Includes examples ____ *Suggested extension: Sing song or rap in front of class ____* Possible points = _____	**6. Collage** Follows Collage criteria card ___ Shows at least 5 ways to document sources ____ Creativity ____ Includes examples ____ Possible points = _____
7. Journal Entry Correct spelling, punctuation and grammar ____ Point of view and feelings are clear ____ Thoughts and decisions show knowledge of laws ____ *Suggested extension: Interview classmates to find out their feelings about this issue. Include in journal ____* Possible points = _____	**8. Debate** Positions on each side are clearly stated ____ Opinions backed up by accurate facts and examples ____ Correct amount of time ____ Uses logic and shows evidence of research ____ *Suggested extension: Present a debate for other classes or entire school ____* Possible points = _____	**9. Time Line** Follows Time Line criteria card __ Shows at least 8 events ____ Correct grammar & spelling ____ At least 3 resources listed ____ *Suggested extension: Write an explanation of why these changes have taken place ____* Possible points = _____

Points for activities: #_____ = _____ pts., #_____ = _____ pts., #_____ = _____ pts.

Name _____ Total points _____ Grade _____

1. Chose a poem and make a **mobile** that shows its theme, important words or symbols and its title.	**2.** Do a **PowerPoint presentation** comparing and contrasting 2 poems written by the same author.	**3.** Write a **letter** to your grandparent (or another older person) explaining similarities and differences between rap and poetry. Include an example of both.
4. Using a digital camera, take pictures that illustrate a poem. Do a **slide show** on the computer combining the pictures with the words of the poem.	**5.** Make a **poster** illustrating these 4 elements of poetry: Theme, Purpose, Mood, Form. Include an explanation of each.	**6.** Choose a poem and put the **words to music**. Sing it for your class.
7. Design a **brochure** advertising a new Poetry Club at your school. Include advantages of being able to read, write and interpret poetry.	**8.** Compile an **illustrated booklet** of 10 poems you have written.	**9.** Make a **scrapbook** of your favorite poems. Write a short **paragraph** for each poem telling why you like it.

I/we chose activities # _____, #_____, and #_____.

Name _____ **Date** _____ **Due date** _____

© Pieces of Learning

1. Mobile	2. PowerPoint	3. Letter
1. Follows Mobile criteria card _____	Follows PowerPoint criteria card _____	Correct letter format _____
Has 5 or more important words or symbols _____	Similarities and differences clearly shown _____	Similarities and differences clearly shown _____
Has title _____	Contains both poems _____	Includes example of each _____
Visuals relate to theme _____	Visuals relate to poems _____	Correct grammar, mechanics and spelling _____
Suggested extension: Include information about poet _____	*Suggested extension: Include information about poet* _____	*Suggested extension: Include several types of music in addition to rap* _____
Possible points = _____	Possible points = _____	Possible points = _____
4. Slide Show	**5. Poster**	**6. Song**
At least 10 pictures _____	Follows Poster criteria card _____	Includes entire poem _____
Pictures relate to words _____	Has all 4 elements _____	Music fits words _____
Includes title and author of poem _____	Illustrations relate to elements _____	Tells title and author of poem _____
Words of poem are accurate and spelled correctly _____	Has explanation of each _____	Words and music are clear and presented well _____
Suggested extension: Include music or speaking in slide show _____	*Suggested extension: Give an example of each element taken from different poems* _____	*Suggested extension: Use instrument or other musical enhancements* _____
Possible points = _____	Possible points = _____	Possible points = _____
7. Brochure	**8. Illustrated Booklet**	**9. Scrapbook**
Follows Brochure criteria card _____	Has 10 poems _____	Has at least 10 poems _____
Lists several advantages of understanding poetry _____	Neat and legible _____	Paragraphs show understanding of poems _____
Uses persuasive words _____	All poems are original _____	Correct grammar, mechanics and spelling _____
Tells purpose of club _____	Illustrations relate to poems _____	Neat and legible _____
Suggested extension: Write brochure in poetic form _____	*Suggested extension: Write more than 10 poems using different poetry styles and patterns* _____	*Suggested extension: Include a variety of styles of poetry from different poets* _____
Possible points = _____	Possible points = _____	Possible points = _____

Points for activities: #_____ = _____ pts., #_____ = _____ pts., #_____ = _____ pts.

Name _____ **Total points** _____ **Grade** _____

1.	2.	3.
Design a rainforest **bookmark**. Include a picture and a message about the rainforest.	**List** 5 trees found in the rainforest. Rank order them beginning with those we should harvest freely and ending with those we should not cut down. Write a **sentence** about each that explains your thinking.	Create a **wordfind** that includes at least 20 words about the rainforest.
(Knowledge)	*(Evaluation)*	*(Knowledge)*
4.	5.	6.
Working with at least 2 of your classmates who have also chosen this activity, make a **mural** of a rainforest along a wall of your classroom or in the hallway of your school. Show 3 or more plants and animals in each layer of the rainforest.	Create a **poster** advertising reasons to save the rainforest.	Using books and the Internet, research animals and plants found in the rainforest. Find one for every letter of the alphabet. Make an illustrated Rainforest **ABC book**.
(Application)	*(Evaluation)*	*(Comprehension)*
7.	8.	9.
Read <u>The Great Kapok Tree</u> by Lynne Cherry. Create a **chart** showing fact and fantasy in the book.	Make a rainforest **diorama**. Include all rainforest layers with representative plants and animals in each layer.	Write a **poem** about the rainforest.
(Analysis)	*(Application)*	*(Synthesis)*

I/we chose activities # _____, #_____, and #_____.

Name _____ **Date** _____ **Due date** _____

1. Bookmark	2. List & Sentences	3. Wordfind
Has a correctly spelled message about the rainforest _____ Picture shows some aspect of the rainforest _____ Visually attractive; appropriate shape and size _____ *Suggested extension: Include title of a rainforest book or website* _____ Possible points = _____	Lists 5 trees in rank order _____ Has a sentence about each tree _____ Reasons are logical and are clearly stated _____ *Suggested extension: Include more than 5 trees* _____ Possible points = _____	Has 20 rainforest words _____ Correct spelling _____ Neat and legible _____ *Suggested extension: Include another paper with definitions of each rainforest word* _____ Possible points = _____
4. Mural	5. Poster	6. ABC Book
Shows 3 or more plants and animals in each layer _____ Accurate illustration of each layer _____ Group cooperation, planning and effort _____ Visually attractive & neat _____ *Suggested extension: Include written explanations and labels* _____ Possible points = _____	Follows Poster criteria card _____ Reasons are clearly stated _____ Reasons are logical and backed up by facts _____ *Suggested extension: Include bibliography of sources attached to poster* _____ Possible points = _____	Has a rainforest plant or animal for every letter _____ Includes name and picture _____ Creativity _____ Accuracy _____ *Suggested extension: Include facts about each on each page of book* _____ Possible points = _____
7. Chart	8. Diorama	9. Poem
Follows Chart criteria card _____ Clearly shows fact and fantasy _____ Accurate information from book _____ *Suggested extension: Compare with another book about the rainforest such as The Lorax* _____ Possible points = _____	Follows Diorama criteria card _____ Includes all layers _____ Has 2-3 plants and animals for each layer _____ *Suggested extension: Include written labels and explanations* _____ Possible points = _____	Follows Poem criteria card _____ Shows knowledge and feelings about the rainforest _____ Creative _____ *Suggested extension: Illustrate your poem* _____ Possible points = _____

Points for activities: #_____ = _____ pts., #_____ = _____ pts., #_____ = _____ pts.

Name _____ **Total points** _____ **Grade** _____

1.	2.	3.
Draw 4 **pictures** showing what an apple tree looks like in Summer, Fall, Winter and Spring.	Use different **shapes** to make people or objects that make you think of each of the 4 seasons. Paste the shapes on 4 sheets of construction paper and write the name of the season at the top of each.	Write a **story** about an animal that hibernates in winter. Draw a **picture** of where it hibernates.
4.	**5.**	**6.**
Show **seasonal locations** by using construction paper circles for the sun and the earth to show where each is located in relationship to the other in summer and in winter.	Make a **chart** with 4 sections. Put the name of one season in each section. List 3 important things about each season in the correct section.	Write and recite a **poem** about your favorite season.
7.	**8.**	**9.** Write a **paragraph** about one of these: *What would happen if . . . it snowed in the summer? *What would happen if . . . the seasons never changed?
Write a **shape story** using a shape from your favorite season.	Make a **word search** of seasonal words.	

I/we chose activities # _____, #_____, and #_____.

Name _____ **Date** _____ **Due date** _____

1. Tree Pictures	**2. Seasonal Shapes**	**3. Illustrated Story**
Differences in seasons clearly shown _____	At least 3 shapes _____	Story has beginning, middle and end _____
Creativity _____	One paper labeled for each season _____	Is about an animal that hibernates _____
Has 4 pictures of trees _____	People or objects from shapes relate correctly to season chosen _____	Correct place drawn _____
Suggested extension: Draw additional pictures of other types of trees in the 4 seasons _____	*Suggested extension: Use more than 3 shapes _____*	Correct sentence structure and spelling _____
Possible points = _____	Possible points = _____	Possible points = _____
4. Seasonal Locations	**5. Chart**	**6. Poem**
Sun and moon labeled _____	Chart has 4 sections with 1 season in each _____	Poem is about a season _____
Correct location _____	3 important things listed for each season _____	At least 6 lines _____
Shows differences in summer and winter _____	*Suggested extension: Include additional unusual facts about the season _____*	Oral presentation is clear with good volume _____
Suggested extension: Explain why summer and winter are reversed in the northern and southern hemispheres _____		*Suggested extension: Put poem to music and sing _____*
Possible points = _____	Possible points = _____	Possible points = _____
7. Shape Story	**8. Word Search**	**9. Paragraph**
Shape relates to story _____	Has 10 words about seasons _____	Paragraph is about 1 of the two questions _____
Story is about a season _____	Correct spelling _____	Shows good thinking and reasoning _____
Has facts or ideas about the season chosen _____	Neat & organized _____	Gives examples _____
Well organized with good sentence structure _____	*Suggested extension: Define words on a separate sheet of paper _____*	Correct sentence structure and spelling _____
Possible points = _____	Possible points = _____	Possible points = _____

Points for activities: #_____ = _____ pts., #_____ = _____ pts., #_____ = _____ pts.

Name _____ Total points _____ Grade _____

1. Write a **story** using shapes as characters. (Example: Ralph Rectangle, Suzy Square) *(Language Arts)*	**2.** Do a **scale drawing** of your dream house. Show the area of each room. Include interesting shapes in your house. *(Math)*	**3.** Draw a detailed **map** of a neighborhood or area. Label important buildings and include the shapes they contain. *(Social Studies)*
4. Create a character named for a shape. Dress like this character and perform a 2-minute **monologue** as this character, telling about yourself and what you like to do. *(Performing arts)*	**5.** Collect 10 natural objects you can find outside. (Examples: leaves, rocks, flowers, etc.) Arrange in a box or other type of **display**. Label each item according to what it is and what shape or shapes it has. *(Science)*	**6.** Create a **design** from cut paper that exhibits positive and negative shapes. *(Visual arts)*
7. Make a list of 20 locations in the United States or the world. Use a U.S. map or world map to locate them, then draw line segments between them in different ways. How many different shapes can you make? Label the **shapes on the map**. *(Social Studies)*	**8.** Find information on the Internet or read a book about quilting. Write a **report** about how shapes are used in making quilts. Include a picture or diagram. *(Language Arts)* *(Visual Arts)*	**9.** Use a **Venn diagram** to compare and contrast geometric shapes and free-form shapes. *(Math)*

I/we chose activities # _____, # _____, and # _____.

Name _____ Date _____ Due date _____

1. Story	**2. Scale Drawing**	**3. Map**
Has at least 3 characters _____	Accurate scale _____	Buildings and shapes labeled _____
At least 2 pages with a beginning, middle and end _____	Area figured correctly _____	Map accurately shows area or neighborhood _____
Characters' actions relate to shapes _____	Has 4 or more shapes _____	Follows Map criteria card _____
Correct grammar, mechanics and spelling _____	Neatly done _____	*Suggested extension: Draw a second map showing improvements you would like to see in the area* _____
Suggested extension: Write longer story that includes illustrations _____	*Suggested extension: Show area around house and include other shapes* _____	
Possible points = _____	Possible points = _____	Possible points = _____
4. Monologue	**5. Display**	**6. Design**
Costume reflects shape _____	Contains 10 natural objects _____	Design visually attractive _____
Monologue has details about the character and his life _____	Correct labels of items and shapes _____	Positive and negative shapes clearly shown _____
Creativity _____	Attractive and neat display _____	*Suggested extension: Write a report explaining positive and negative shapes* _____
Follows Oral Presentation criteria card _____	*Suggested extensions: Include other facts about objects; label more than 10 objects* _____	
Suggested extension: Include visuals and props _____		
Possible points = _____	Possible points = _____	Possible points = _____
7. Map Shapes	**8. Report & Visual**	**9. Venn Diagram**
List has 20 different locations, either U.S. or world _____	Report explains information learned from book or Internet _____	Similarities and differences clearly shown _____
Correct locations of each clearly indicated on map _____	Correct grammar, mechanics and spelling _____	At least 3 ideas on each section of Venn diagram _____
At least 5 different shapes _____	Well organized _____	Accurate information _____
Shapes labeled correctly _____	Has visual of quilt shapes _____	Neat and legible _____
Suggested extension: Include more than 20 locations and more than 5 shapes _____	*Suggested extension: Make quilt piece from various shapes* _____	*Suggested extension: Include visuals of each type* _____
Possible points = _____	Possible points = _____	Possible points = _____

Points for activities: #_____ = _____ pts.,   #_____ = _____ pts.,   #_____ = _____ pts.

Name _____ Total points _____ Grade _____

1. On a world **map**, locate 5 deserts and label each. Find out what kinds of plants grow in deserts. **Draw and label** 5 desert plants at the bottom of your map. *(Sand)*	**2.** Find out about different cultures that make sand paintings. Write a **paragraph** about this art form and make your own **sand painting**. *(Sand)*	**3.** Write a **poem or short story** about what it is like to walk and play on sand at the beach or build a sand castle. *(Sand)*
4. Research how adobe brick is made. Make a **mural** showing the process Indians used to make adobe brick and how they built their houses. *(Clay)*	**5.** Find out about different cultures that are known for their clay pottery. Write a **paragraph** about this art form and make your own **pottery** out of clay. *(Clay)*	**6.** Write a **poem or story** about someone who takes a mud bath or has a mudpack on his or her face. Be sure to describe what it would feel like! *(Clay)*
7. Find out about the role of worms in the process of composting. Create a **comic strip** that shows at least 6 things worms can do in soil. *(Humus)*	**8.** Make a **Venn Diagram** comparing and contrasting Composting and Recycling. *(Humus)*	**9.** Write a **short story** titled "A Day in My Life in the Compost Pile". Write from the point of view of an insect or worm. *(Humus)*

I/we chose activities # _____, # _____, and # _____.

Name _____ Date _____ Due date _____

Assessment
Soil Tic-Tac-Toe

1. Map & Drawings	2. Paragraph & Painting	3. Poem
Has 5 deserts correctly located on world map _____ 5 desert plants correctly drawn and labeled _____ *Suggested extension: Write a paragraph explaining why these plants grow well in sandy soil* _____ Possible points = _____	Paragraph explains how sand paintings are done _____ Cultures that make sand paintings are discussed _____ Correct spelling, mechanics and grammar _____ Painting neat and attractive _____ *Suggested extension: Paint in Native American style* _____ Possible points = _____	Correct writing style for poem or story _____ Has at least 10 descriptive words _____ Explanation is clear _____ *Suggested extension: Write another paragraph comparing walking on sand and walking on quicksand* _____ Possible points = _____
4. Mural	**5. Paragraph & Pottery**	**6. Poem or Story**
Shows knowledge about making adobe brick _____ Shows typical adobe house _____ Originality/creativity _____ Follows Mural criteria card _____ *Suggested extension: Write report about how adobe is made and some of the cultures that used it* _____ Possible points = _____	Paragraph explains clay pottery as an art form _____ Correct grammar, mechanics and spelling _____ Pottery well constructed _____ Pottery is decorated _____ *Suggested extension: Make pottery in style of a certain culture* _____ Possible points = _____	Explains how this mud is made and what it is made of _____ Includes descriptions of how it feels _____ Correct writing style for poem or story _____ *Suggested extension: Draw a picture illustrating your poem or story* _____ Possible points = _____
7. Comic Strip	**8. Venn Diagram**	**9. Short Story**
Follows Comic Strip criteria card _____ Creativity _____ Shows 6 different things worms can do _____ Accurate information _____ *Suggested extension: Include other soil creatures in comic strip* _____ Possible points = _____	Has accurate facts and details about both _____ Similarities and differences clearly shown _____ Clear labels and writing _____ Well organized _____ *Suggested extension: Make a 3-circle Venn diagram with Stripping the Land of Trees included* _____ Possible points = _____	Story has a beginning, middle and end _____ Accurate information _____ Point of view clear _____ Includes descriptions of things in compost pile _____ *Suggested extension: Include 2 or more different characters* _____ Possible points = _____

Points for activities: #_____ = _____ pts.,   #_____ = _____ pts.,   #_____ = _____ pts.

Name _____ Total points _____ Grade _____

1. In the 1500s, the Inca town of Machu Picchu was destroyed by the Spanish. The ruins were discovered in 1911. Find out about Machu Picchu. Then pretend you are an explorer who discovers the ruins. Write a **letter** to your friends at home telling about your discovery.	**2.** On a map of South America, use the scale to measure the distances between any 4 capital cities. Make a **chart** to record your information. Then use a map of your country and find 4 cities approximately the same distances from where you live. Record this information on your chart.	**3.** Create **Jeopardy questions** about South America. Include 5 categories of questions with 5 questions in each category. Write your questions and answers on index cards.
4. Make a **Venn diagram** comparing and contrasting the Amazon rainforest and the Atacama Desert.	**5.** Write a **poem** about any topic that relates to South America's weather, landforms or climate.	**6.** Create a **mosaic** showing a typical village scene in South America.
7. Write an **editorial** explaining your point of view about any current political issue in 1 South American country.	**8.** Choose any country in South America. Create a **brochure** advertising it to tourists.	**9.** 2 interesting islands in South America are the Galapogos Islands and Easter Island. Research 1 of these and do an **oral report** for the class explaining what you find out. Include **visuals**.

I/we chose activities # _____, #_____, and #_____.

Name _____ **Date** _____ **Due date** _____

1. Letter Has correct grammar, punctuation and spelling _____ Explains what the ruins looked like in 1911 _____ Accurate information _____ Well-written descriptions _____ *Suggested extension: Include pictures of Machu Picchu* _____ Possible points = _____	**2. Chart** Follows Chart criteria card _____ Accurate measurements _____ Accurate information _____ Correct spelling, punctuation and grammar _____ *Suggested extension: Write conclusions based on information on chart* _____ Possible points = _____	**3. Jeopardy questions** Has 25 questions in 5 categories _____ Accurate information _____ Neatly written _____ *Suggested extension: Organize a Jeopardy game for 3 classmates using your questions* _____ Possible points = _____
4. Venn Diagram Follows Venn Diagram criteria card _____ Clearly shows similarities and differences _____ Accurate information _____ *Suggested extension: Include another South American landform and do a Venn Diagram with 3 circles* _____ Possible points = _____	**5. Poem** Follows Poem criteria card _____ Accurate information _____ Includes examples _____ Relates to topic _____ *Suggested extensions: Recite poem in front of class; illustrate poem showing your knowledge of topic* _____ Possible points = _____	**6. Mosaic** Follows Mosaic criteria card _____ Clearly shows village _____ Creativity _____ Looks like a South American village _____ *Suggested extension: Include factual information about a village* _____ Possible points = _____
7. Editorial Correct spelling, punctuation and grammar _____ Point of view is clear _____ Accurate information about political issue _____ Logical reasons given to support point of view _____ *Suggested extension: Write 2 editorials on the topic with 2 different points of view* _____ Possible points = _____	**8. Brochure** Follows Brochure criteria card _____ Highlights important sights in chosen country _____ Includes a map _____ Uses persuasive language _____ *Suggested extension: Figure out the cost of visiting these places* _____ Possible points = _____	**9. Oral Report with Visuals** Follows Oral Report criteria card _____ Accurate information _____ Clear and colorful visuals that add to presentation _____ At least 3 resources used _____ *Suggested extension: Tell how you could travel there and what the cost and time would be* _____ Possible points = _____

Points for activities: #_____ = _____ pts.,   #_____ = _____ pts.,   #_____ = _____ pts.

Name _____ Total points _____ Grade _____

Stock Market
Tic-Tac-Toe for Student Choice Activities

1. Create a **board game** with a stock market theme. Play it with a group of friends. *(Bodily/Kinesthetic)*	**2.** Make a **chart** comparing and contrasting a "dot.com" stock with a food company stock. Write a **paragraph** explaining their similarities and differences. *(Mathematical/Logical)*	**3.** Follow 3 stocks for one week. **Visually present** the movement of each in a different way. *(Visual/Spatial)*
4. **Interview** 3 people who have invested in the stock market sometime within the last 10 years. Find out what their experiences were and how they feel about the stock market now. Write a **paper** explaining your conclusions. *(Intrapersonal)*	**5.** Write a **musical jingle** advertising a brokerage firm. Sing it for the class or record it on tape. *(Musical/Rhythmic)*	**6.** Make a **list** of 10 environmentally friendly stocks. Write a **sentence** defending each of your choices. *(Naturalist)*
7. Lead a **class discussion** on the pros and cons of investing in the stock market. *(Interpersonal)*	**8.** Make a **crossword puzzle** using stock market words and jargon. *(Verbal/Linguistic)*	**9.** Choose a stock and **graph** its earnings for one week. Write a **paragraph** explaining its movement. *(Mathematical/Logical)*

I/we chose activities # _____, #_____, and #_____.

Name _____ Date _____ Due date _____

1. Board Game	**2. Chart & Paragraph**	**3. Visuals**
Follows Game criteria card _____ Includes at least 20 different facts or stocks _____ Facts are accurate and relate to stock market _____ *Suggested extensions: Include more than 20 stocks and little-known or unusual facts; Make game unusual and challenging* _____ Possible points = _____	Clear explanation _____ Follows Chart criteria card _____ Correct spelling, punctuation and grammar _____ Shows similarities and differences _____ *Suggested extension: Write a paragraph defending which stock is better* _____ Possible points = _____	3 clear visuals _____ Accurate information _____ Each visual is different _____ Neat and visually pleasing _____ *Suggested extensions: Use more than 3 stocks; include different types of stocks* _____ Possible points = _____
4. Interview & Paper	**5. Musical Jingle**	**6. List & Sentences**
Interviewed 3 people _____ Interview responses and notes written or recorded _____ Feelings and conclusions summarized clearly _____ Correct spelling, grammar and mechanics _____ *Suggested extension: Interview more than 3 people with different experiences* _____ Possible points = _____	Follows Song criteria card _____ Includes reasons for using this brokerage firm _____ Accurate information about brokerage firm chosen _____ *Suggested extension: Teach the song to the class and have them sing it with you* _____ Possible points = _____	Includes 10 or more stocks _____ Explains why each is environmentally friendly _____ Accurate information _____ *Suggested extension: Make another list of 10 environmentally unfriendly stocks and defend your choices* _____ Possible points = _____
7. Class Discussion	**8. Crossword Puzzle**	**9. Graph & Paragraph**
Has prepared discussion questions to ask class _____ Knows both pros and cons _____ Clearly explains opinions _____ Allows both sides equal time to be heard _____ *Suggested extension: Write a summary of both viewpoints and reasons for each* _____ Possible points = _____	Follows Crossword Puzzle criteria card _____ Has at least 20 words related to the stock market _____ Well organized _____ *Suggested extensions: Use stock market abbreviations with correct definitions* _____ Possible points = _____	Follows Graph criteria card _____ Accurate information _____ Explanation is logical and reflects knowledge of stock _____ Correct grammar, spelling and mechanics _____ *Suggested extension: Choose 2 or more stocks* _____ Possible points = _____

Points for activities: #_____ = _____ pts.,   #_____ = _____ pts.,   #_____ = _____ pts.

Name _____   Total points _____   Grade _____

1.	**2.**	**3.**
Make a **sculpture** of a Native American thunderbird. Include a **card** displayed beside the sculpture that explains the myths and legends about the thunderbird. *(Bodily/Kinesthetic)*	Make an **oral presentation** explaining why weather is so important to people who work in agriculture. Give at least 3 examples. *(Verbal/Linguistic)*	Find out ways animals can be good predictors of weather. Show your findings on a **poster**. Include at least 5 examples. *(Naturalist)*
4.	**5.**	**6.**
Work with a group of at least 2 other classmates to produce a **world weather map** with at least 10 weather symbols. Each person should be responsible for part of the project. *(Interpersonal)*	Find at least 5 **songs** that relate to weather. Make a copy of the words and music. Sing or play 1 of them for the class. *(Musical/Rhythmic)*	Make a **collage** showing different kinds of storms. Label each. *(Visual/Spatial)*
7.	**8.**	**9.**
Write a 2-week **journal** reflecting on your moods and feelings during different types of weather. Write a conclusion about the relationship between weather and moods. *(Intrapersonal)*	Make a **mobile** of 5 different weather instruments. Hang a card beside each to explain what it is and what it measures. *(Bodily/Kinesthetic)*	Figure out the percentage of sunny, cloudy, snowy and rainy days in your town during the past month. Compare this to the same month last year. Show your **calculations** and write **conclusions** you can make based on this information. *(Logical/Mathematical)*

I/we chose activities # _____, #_____, and #_____.

Name _____ **Date** _____ **Due date** _____

1. Sculpture & Card Realistic thunderbird ____ Sturdy and neat ____ Accurate information ____ Myths clearly explained ____ *Suggested extension: Explain similar myths in other cultures* ____ Possible points = _____	**2. Oral Presentation** Follows Oral Report criteria card ____ Includes 3 examples ____ Accurate information ____ Logical reasons ____ *Suggested extension: Use visuals to go along with report* ____ Possible points = _____	**3. Poster** Follows Poster criteria card ____ Has 5 examples ____ Logical explanation ____ Accurate information ____ *Suggested extension: Explore myths about animals and weather from other cultures* ____ Possible points = _____
4. World Weather Map Follows Map criteria card ____ Group cooperation ____ Accurate information ____ At least 10 symbols ____ *Suggested extension: Do a TV weather report using map* ____ Possible points = _____	**5. Songs** Follows Song criteria card ____ Has 5 or more songs that relate to weather ____ Presents song to class ____ *Suggested extension: Make booklet with illustrations of each song* ____ Possible points = _____	**6. Collage** Follows Collage criteria card ____ Has 5 or more different types of storms ____ Accurate labels ____ *Suggested extension: Show geographical locations for different types of storms* ____ Possible points = _____
7. Journal Daily entries for 2 weeks ____ Shows relationship between weather and moods ____ Clear conclusions ____ Correct spelling, punctuation and grammar ____ *Suggested extension: Interview another person to see if their weather moods are the same as yours* ____ Possible points = _____	**8. Mobile** Follows Mobile criteria card ____ Has 5 different weather instruments ____ Has 5 explanations ____ Accurate information ____ *Suggested extension: Use more than 5 instruments* ____ Possible points = _____	**9. Calculations** Shows all data and calculations ____ Accuracy ____ Conclusions are logical ____ Sources of information are listed ____ *Suggested extension: Include different climates and areas throughout the world* ____ Possible points = _____

Points for activities: #_____ = _____ pts., #_____ = _____ pts., #_____ = _____ pts.

Name _____ Total points _____ Grade _____

1. Write a **poem** about an historic World War II event or about someone's life and feelings during that time period *(Easiest)*	**2.** Make a **crossword puzzle** using at least 20 words related to World War II. *(Easiest)*	**3.** Make a **collage** about an event or battle during World War II. Use different types of pictures and materials. Include written facts about the event or battle. *(Easiest)*
4. Organize and lead a **Quiz Bowl** on World War II. *(More Difficult)*	**5.** Draw a **map** showing countries and major battles in Europe/Africa or in Asia and the Pacific during World War II. *(More Difficult)*	**6.** Build a **model airplane** from the 1939-1945 time period. *(More Difficult)*
7. Write and direct a **one-act play** depicting an event from World War II. Choose classmates to act in the play and perform it for the class. *(Most Difficult)*	**8.** Make a 5-minute **video** recreating an important event in World War II. *(Most Difficult)*	**9.** Read a book about a battle or battles during World War II. Give an **oral report** that includes maps and other visuals. *(Most Difficult)*

I/we chose activities # _____, # _____, and # _____.

Name _____ Date _____ Due date _____

1. Poem	2. Crossword Puzzle	3. Collage
Follows Poem criteria card _____ Historically accurate _____ *Suggested extension: Include illustration depicting the poem _____* Possible points = _____	Has 20 words connected to World War II _____ Follows Crossword Puzzle criteria card _____ *Suggested extension: Make shape of puzzle reflect topic _____* Possible points = _____	Follows Collage criteria card _____ Clearly shows an event or battle _____ Facts included on collage or on back of paper _____ *Suggested extension: Design a time line of the event or battle shown in the collage _____* Possible points = _____
4. Quiz Bowl	5. Map	6. Model Airplane
Has at least 25 questions with correct answers about World War II _____ Clear rules for participants _____ Well organized _____ *Suggested extension: Create additional challenge questions for finalists or winners _____* Possible points = _____	Follows Map criteria card _____ Historically accurate _____ Shows both countries and battles _____ *Suggested extension: Make a chart comparing and contrasting this map with a present-day map of the same region _____* Possible points = _____	Follows Model criteria card _____ Historically accurate details _____ Includes display card with significant and interesting facts and details about this airplane _____ *Suggested extension: Include a diorama or other type of scenery to show location and setting for plane _____* Possible points = _____
7. One-Act Play	8. Video	9. Oral Report
Follows Script criteria card _____ Well organized performance _____ Historically accurate _____ Has props and costumes _____ *Suggested extension: Make the writer the narrator and fill in historical details for audience _____* Possible points = _____	Follows Video criteria card _____ Historically accurate _____ Has several important details about the event _____ Well organized _____ *Suggested extension: Use special effects or music in the video _____* Possible points = _____	Follows Oral Report criteria card _____ Book is on proper reading level _____ Clear and accurate visuals _____ Accurate summary of battles _____ *Suggested extension: Compare to battles in other wars _____* Possible points = _____

Points for activities: #_____ = _____ pts., #_____ = _____ pts., #_____ = _____ pts.

Name _____ **Total points** _____ **Grade** _____

Tic-Tac-Toe activities are user-friendly and easy to write. Use this format for any grade level and with any subject or content. Follow the steps below as you learn to write both activities and assessments using this format.

___1. Decide on a major theme, focus or topic for the student activities. This may be in conjunction with a certain unit of study, or it may be generic, such as a spelling Tic-Tac-Toe that could be used with spelling words for several weeks.

___2. Look at your state standards in one or more subject areas to give you a focus for the activities you will write.

___3. Start writing as many activities as you can think of that correlate with the standards and/or topic. Write each activity on separate small Post-it® notes.

___4. Place the Post-it® notes with the activities on a blank Tic-Tac-Toe grid in any order. You will find a blank form on page 77 and on the *Activities and Assessments* CD.

___5. Check the configuration of the activities on the grid. Move the Post-it® notes around until you get the student choices in appropriate positions so that no matter which way students choose, they will be doing the variety of activities you desire.

___6. You may want to categorize the activities according to Multiple Intelligences, Learning Modalities, Learning Styles, Bloom's Taxonomy, subject areas, etc. Look for many different examples in the Tic-Tac-Toe grids in this book.

___7. When you have all activities in the desired order, write or type them onto a Tic-Tac-Toe grid.

___8. If you develop a Tic-Tac-Toe and decide some of the activities in it are too difficult or too easy for some of your students, substitute a more appropriate activity or activities as needed. Many times you will only need to change one or two activities out of the nine to make a more difficult or less difficult version of the Tic-Tac-Toe. You could end up with tiered Tic-Tac-Toes, all of which focus on the same topic but with slightly different activities.

___9. Write an easy-to-understand checklist of assessment criteria for each of the activities. Put the criteria into a Tic-Tac-Toe assessment grid, with the criteria corresponding to the number of the activity. Include points as desired. You will find a blank form to use on page 78 and on the *Activities and Assessments* CD.

___10. List standards covered on the Tic-Tac-Toe form itself or on a separate page.

Tic-Tac-Toe for Student Choice Activities

_____

1.	2.	3.
4.	5.	6
7.	8.	9.

Name _____ I chose activities #_____, #_____, #_____.

Date _____ Due date _____

_____ Tic-Tac-Toe

1.	2.	3.
4.	5.	6.
7.	8.	9.

Points for Activities: #____ = ____ pts., #____ = ____ pts., #____ = ____ pts.

Name _____ **Total points** _____ **Grade** _____ **Comments:**

Individual Lesson Plans in the *Teaching Tools* Format

The *Teaching Tools* Individual Lesson Plans (ILP) are units of work. They are called Individual Lesson Plans because students create their own individual plans by choosing one or more of the *Student Choice Activities*. (Individual Lesson Plans are written using the format found in *Teaching Tools for the 21st Century*, Pieces of Learning, publisher.)

This section contains 10 *Teaching Tools* Individual Lesson Plan units. Each unit has an Individual Lesson Plan with 3 *Required Activities* and 8 *Student Choice Activities*. The *Student Choice Activities* are categorized in various ways – by Learning Modalities, Learning Styles, or Bloom's Taxonomy. There is a corresponding page for each Topic with assessment criteria for each of the *Student Choice Activities*.

The following *Teaching Tools* Individual Lesson Plan units with corresponding assessments are:

How to Use the *Teaching Tools* Individual Lesson Plans with Your Students

When using a *Teaching Tools* Individual Lesson Plan (ILP) give a copy of the plan to each student. All students must complete the *Required Activities* listed in the upper right section of the form. Students choose activities from the *Student Choices* in the 4 blocks in the left section.

They indicate their choices by placing the numbers of the activities or projects on the appropriate lines in the box *Student Choices in Way to Learn*. Students write what they have to turn in or do in the *Product/Performance Student Choice* box.

Ancient Egypt (page 81) is an example of how ILP's work. In this example, the student will complete the 3 *Required Activities* plus make a model of a pyramid (Choice #2) and create a mythical creature and write a description (Choice #6).

The teacher decides how many *Student Choice Activities* each student must do. Begin by requiring students to make 2 choices, each from a different category. If students finish early, they can make an additional choice.

To know which activities students have chosen, record the numbers of the *Student Choices* each student makes. (example page 82) Use the blank form on page 83 for your students or use the form on the *Activities and Assessments* CD. Meet with all the students who are doing the same activity to review assessment criteria, due dates, etc. Do this for each of the *Student Choice Activities*.

Plan the due dates carefully. Activities such as debates or oral reports need class time for preparation and presentation. Make sure everything is not due on the same day! This avoids student procrastination and makes grading less overwhelming for you. It helps you space these events throughout the week or weeks the student are working. It also assures oral reports and other classroom presentations are spaced over several days.

Begin by trying one of the *Teaching Tools ILP's*. Then, using the guidelines on page 104 write one of your own. There are blank forms for you to use both in the book (pages 105-111) and on the *Activities and Assessments* CD:

Individual Lesson Plan – Learning Modalities (page 106)

Assessment of ILP – Learning Modalities (page 107)

Individual Lesson Plan – Learning Styles (page 108)

Assessment of ILP – Learning Styles (page 109)

Individual Lesson Plan – Bloom's Taxonomy (page 110)

Assessment of ILP – Bloom's Taxonomy (page 111)

Individual Lesson Plan – Multiple Intelligences (pages 112, 114)

Assessment of ILP – Multiple Intelligences (pages 113, 115)

Sample Individual Lesson Plan – Ancient Egypt

Required Activities Teacher's Choice	Product/Performance Required	Assessment – Required Activities
1. Read a book about some aspect of Ancient Egypt. (Assigned by the teacher or chosen by the student.)	1. Contributions to class or small group discussion	1. Informal observations during class discussion
2. Develop an outline of the people and their jobs building the pyramids.	2. Outline	2. Accuracy Organization Eight or more jobs listed
3. View a video about ancient Egypt. Write a summary.	3. Summary	3. Includes important details Clarity of thought Correct spelling, grammar, punctuation

Optional Student-Parent Cooperative Activity

Work together on the Ancient Egypt Webquest.

Student Choices in Ways to Learn	Product/Performance Student Choice	Due Dates Student Choice Activities
Application 2	2. Model of pyramid	
Analysis		
Synthesis 6	6. Mythical creature and written description	
Evaluation		

ACTIVITIES – STUDENT CHOICES

Application	Synthesis
1. Draw a diagram depicting the location of the items in King Tut's tomb.	5. Pretend you have been chosen to interview King Tut about the circumstances of his death. Develop six interview questions and possible answers he might have given.
2. Make a model of an Egyptian pyramid. Include both the outer walls and inner chambers.	6. Create a mythical creature that is part animal and part human. Draw it and write a description of its many powers.

Analysis	Evaluation
3. Make a chart comparing and contrasting the tools used in building ancient Egyptian pyramids and tools used to build modern buildings.	7. Write an editorial giving your viewpoint about the following: Which is better – burial in a cemetery or in a pyramid? Defend your point of view.
4. Design a plan for keeping looters out of ancient Egyptian tombs. Include written plans and diagrams as needed.	8. Evaluate the importance of the Nile River to the Ancient Egyptians. Use charts, graphs, facts and figures to show its importance.

Activity Chart

Student Choice Activities

Students' Names	1	2	3	4	5	6	7	8
Alicia		✓			✓			
Carlos				✓			✓	
Danielle	✓					✓		
Evan			✓					✓
Edwardo				✓		✓		
Gina		✓					✓	
Heather						✓	✓	
Jim			✓			✓		
Kara	✓							✓
Maria			✓			✓		
Mark		✓			✓			
Nathan	✓					✓		
Ophra			✓					✓
Paul		✓				✓		
Pedro				✓			✓	
Quintan	✓							✓
Rachel				✓		✓		
Rusty					✓		✓	
Sarah	✓			✓				
Taneka		✓						✓
Tom				✓			✓	

Using this chart helps teachers organize a differentiated classroom. Each student in this example chose 2 activities from the 8 Student Choice Activities available. Each child's choices are recorded by using the number that corresponds to the activity.

The teacher meets with each group of students. At this time, review the assessment criteria, explain the activity, and schedule the due date. Record the due date on the chart and also write it in the teacher's plan book. If the activity is one that requires students working together, review behavioral guidelines with the students involved.

Activity Chart

Student Choice Activities

Students' Names	1	2	3	4	5	6	7	8

Notes

Individual Lesson Plan – Ancient Egypt

ACTIVITIES – STUDENT CHOICES

Application	Synthesis
1. Draw a diagram depicting the location of the items in King Tut's tomb. 2. Make a model of an Egyptian pyramid. Include both the outer walls and inner chambers.	5. Pretend you have been chosen to interview King Tut about the circumstances of his death. Develop six interview questions and possible answers he might have given. 6. Create a mythical creature that is part animal and part human. Draw it and write a description of its many powers.
Analysis	**Evaluation**
3. Make a chart comparing and contrasting the tools used in building ancient Egyptian pyramids and tools used to build modern buildings. 4. Design a plan for keeping looters out of ancient Egyptian tombs. Include written plans and diagrams as needed.	7. Write an editorial giving your viewpoint about the following: Which is better – burial in a cemetery or in a pyramid? Defend your point of view. 8. Evaluate the importance of the Nile River to the Ancient Egyptians. Use charts, graphs, facts and figures to show its importance.

Required Activities Teacher's Choice	Product/Performance Required	Assessment – Required Activities
1. Read a book about some aspect of Ancient Egypt. (Assigned by the teacher or chosen by the student.)	1. Contributions to class or small group discussion	1. Informal observations during class discussion
2. Develop an outline of the people and their jobs building the pyramids.	2. Outline	2. Accuracy Organization Eight or more jobs listed
3. View a video about ancient Egypt. Write a summary.	3. Summary	3. Includes important details Clarity of thought Correct spelling, grammar, punctuation

Optional Student-Parent Cooperative Activity

Work together on the Ancient Egypt Webquest.

Student Choices in Ways to Learn	Product/Performance Student Choice	Due Dates Student Choice Activities
Application ______		
Analysis ______		
Synthesis ______		
Evaluation ______		

© Carolyn Coil, www.carolyncoil.com

© Pieces of Learning

Assessment of Student Choices – Ancient Egypt Individual Lesson Plan

1. Diagram (Application)

- Follows Diagram criteria card ___
- Historically accurate ___
- Shows a variety of different items ___

Suggested extension: Write an explanation of uses of items. ___

Possible points = ___

2. Model (Application)

- Follows Model criteria card ___
- Includes inside and outside of pyramid ___
- Shows historically accurate details ___

Suggested extension: Compare to pyramid in another culture. ___

Possible points = ___

3. Chart (Analysis)

- Follows Chart criteria card ___
- Clearly shows similarities and differences ___
- Includes conclusions about ancient and modern tools ___

Suggested extension: Include both pictures and words on the chart. ___

Possible points = ___

4. Written Plans & Diagrams (Analysis)

- Plan is realistic, creative and shows logical thinking ___
- Written plan is logical and clear ___
- Correct spelling, grammar and mechanics ___
- Diagrams support and show details of written plan ___

Suggested extension: Make a report to the class about your plan. Include visuals. ___

Possible points = ___

5. Interview Questions & Answers (Synthesis)

- Has 6 or more interview questions ___
- Questions require in-depth, detailed answers ___
- Answers are historically correct and feasible ___

Suggested extension: Write a newspaper article based on these questions and answers. ___

Possible points = ___

6. Mythical Creature (Synthesis)

- Follows Drawing criteria card ___
- Creative and unique mythical creature ___
- Clearly written description ___

Suggested extension: Write a story with your creature as the main character. ___

Possible points = ___

7. Editorial (Evaluation)

- Gives 3 or more reasons to support point of view ___
- Includes factual and accurate information and examples ___
- Well written using persuasive language ___
- Correct grammar, spelling and punctuation ___

Suggested extension: Create an Egyptian newspaper with several articles including your editorial. ___

Possible points = ___

8. Evaluation of Importance of Nile (Evaluation)

- Visuals show information neatly and clearly ___
- Accurate information showing why the Nile is important ___
- Information includes statistics and numbers ___

Suggested extension: Compare the Nile to another important river in the world. ___

Possible points = ___

Individual Lesson Plan – Civil War

Required Activities Teacher's Choice	Product/Performance Required	Assessment – Required Activities
1. Read the textbook about the causes and events of the Civil War. Take notes and make a time line of important events.	1. Notes Time line	1. Accurate and complete notes At least 10 events on time line Follows time line criteria card
2. Make a map of the states during the Civil War. Color code to show North and South. Label locations of important battles.	2. Map	2. Map is accurate and color coded correctly Ten battle locations on map

Optional Student-Parent Cooperative Activity

Student Choices in Ways to Learn	Product/Performance Student Choice	Due Dates Student Choice Activities
Concrete Sequential ____		
Abstract Sequential ____		
Concrete Random ____		
Abstract Random ____		

ACTIVITIES – STUDENT CHOICES

Concrete Sequential	Concrete Random
1. Create a graph comparing the North and the South. Compare numbers of people, soldiers, factories, farms and other important facts.	5. Make a diorama showing the battle between the *Monitor* and the *Merrimac*. Include a paragraph telling about the battle.
2. Research Civil War recruitment posters. Design one of your own that shows some of the causes of the Civil War.	6. Research popular clothing during the Civil War. Make a boy and a girl paper doll and at least three outfits for each.

Abstract Sequential	Abstract Random
3. Rewrite the Gettysburg Address in your own words.	7. Pretend it is 1860. With another classmate, debate why the South should or should not secede from the Union. Include differences in views on states rights, economics and slavery.
4. Research a famous person from the Civil War. Make a PowerPoint presentation about his/her life.	8. Dress as Jefferson Davis or Abraham Lincoln and explain your point of view about the Civil War. You have five minutes to make your case!

© Carolyn Coil, www.carolyncoil.com

86

© Pieces of Learning

Assessment of Student Choices – Civil War Individual Lesson Plan

1. Graph (Concrete Sequential)	5. Diorama (Concrete Random)
• Follows Graph criteria card ___ • Compares people, soldiers, factories and farms ___ • Accuracy ___ *Suggested extension: Write your conclusions based on this information.* ___ Possible points = ___	• Follows Diorama criteria card ___ • Historically accurate representation of each ship ___ • Paragraph is factual and tells about battle ___ *Suggested extension: Tell class details about the battle that couldn't be shown in your diorama.* Possible points = ___
2. Poster (Concrete Sequential)	6. Paper Dolls (Concrete Random)
• Follows Poster criteria card ___ • Shows causes of war ___ • Persuasive language ___ *Suggested extension: Design another poster that is an anti-war poster.* ___ Possible points = ___	• Boy and girl dolls are made with a sturdy material ___ • Clothing is historically accurate ___ • Has three costumes for each doll ___ • Good visual details and neatly done ___ Possible points = ___
3. Rewrite of Gettysburg Address (Abstract Sequential)	7. Debate (Abstract Random)
• Includes all major points made in the original ___ • Uses language that most at your grade level could understand ___ • Correct spelling, grammar and mechanics ___ *Suggested extension: Recite your Gettysburg Address for your class.* ___ Possible points = ___	• Follows Debate criteria card ___ • Accurate information ___ • States rights, economics and slavery are included ___ *Suggested extension: Debate for another class and answer their questions.* ___ Possible points = ___
4. Powerpoint Presentation (Abstract Sequential)	8. Costumed Monologue (Abstract Random)
• Follows Powerpoint criteria card ___ • Accurate information ___ • Includes at least 10 major points about person's life ___ *Suggested extension: Share presentation with another class and answer questions as asked.* ___ Possible points = ___	• Costume historically accurate and looks like person represented ___ • Point of view is clear ___ • Accurate information ___ • Observes time limit ___ Possible points = ___

Individual Lesson Plan – Election Campaigns

ACTIVITIES – STUDENT CHOICES

Application	Synthesis
1. Track polls of voter opinions on the issues. Create charts or graphs showing percentages of opinions on various issues.	5. Give a campaign speech to your class as if you are one of the candidates. Be true to the candidate in the positions you take.
2. Draw or paint a mural showing an important event or issue from a previous election. Be historically accurate.	6. Organize a candidate forum where you role-play one of the candidates. (At least one other person must select this choice.)

Analysis	Evaluation
3. Do a concept map or web showing the interrelationships of issues and candidates.	7. Locate each candidate's website. Identify fact and propaganda in each. Show your conclusions on a chart, giving examples to back up your opinion.
4. Develop a map of voter precincts showing areas with people most likely to vote and areas with people least likely to vote. Analyze reasons for this and write in essay form.	8. Write a newspaper editorial giving your opinions about the election process and issues involved. Give good reasons to support your opinions.

Required Activities Teacher's Choice	Product/Performance Required	Assessment – Required Activities
1. Research at least three candidates' positions on any 4 major issues.	1. Separate page of notes for each issue with sources listed	1. Accuracy Notes relate to issues Has 4 major issues
2. Develop a "Pro" and "Con" chart for each issue.	2. Chart	2. Issues clear Pros and cons listed for each issue
3. Write a paper explaining your point of view on each issue. Give at least three reasons to support your point of view.	3. Written paper	3. Has 3 or more reasons Clarity of thought Correct spelling, grammar, punctuation

Optional Student-Parent Cooperative Activity

Student Choices in Ways to Learn	Product/Performance Student Choice	Due Dates Student Choice Activities
Application _____		
Analysis _____		
Synthesis _____		
Evaluation _____		

© Carolyn Coil, www.carolyncoil.com

Assessment of Student Choices – Election Campaigns Individual Lesson Plan

5. Campaign Speech (Synthesis)

- Follows Oral Report criteria card ____
- Positions are clearly stated and are accurate for candidate ____
- Is enthusiastic and uses persuasive language ____

Suggested extension: Use campaign posters, buttons or other items to capture voter attention. ____

Possible points = ____

6. Candidate Forum (Synthesis)

- Follows Oral Report criteria card ____
- Organized in a fair manner ____
- Positions of each candidate are heard ____

Suggested extension: Videotape forum for school TV show or invite other classes to attend the forum. ____

Possible points = ____

7. Fact & Propaganda Chart (Evaluation)

- Information is accurate as taken from website ____
- Follows Chart criteria card ____
- Has conclusions with examples from website ____
- Correct grammar, spelling and punctuation ____

Suggested extension: Email each candidate sharing your conclusions. Print your emails and responses.

Possible points = ____

8. Editorial (Evaluation)

- Opinions are supported by reasons and facts ____
- Accurate information ____
- Correct spelling, punctuation and grammar ____

Suggested extension: Send your editorial to a local paper.

Possible points = ____

1. Chart or Graph (Application)

- Follows Chart or Graph criteria card ____
- Data is accurate ____
- Sources of data shown ____
- Uses at least four different polls ____

Possible points = ____

2. Mural (Application)

- Follows Mural criteria card ____
- Issue or event illustrated is clear ____
- Shows historically accurate details ____

Suggested extension: Write a report to accompany mural. ____

Possible points = ____

3. Map or Web (Analysis)

- Clear and neat visual ____
- Clearly shows interrelationships of issues ____
- Includes at least three issues and three candidates ____

Suggested extension: Write an essay or opinion paper on the issues shown. ____

Possible points = ____

4. Map & Essay (Analysis)

- Map is clear and shows accurate information ____
- At least three reasons given for voting patterns ____
- Correct spelling, grammar and mechanics ____
- Reasons supported by facts and examples ____

Suggested extension: Write a letter to the candidates sharing your conclusions. ____

Possible points = ____

Individual Lesson Plan – Geometric Shapes

Required Activities Teacher's Choice	Product/Performance Required	Assessment – Required Activities
1. Define and label basic geometric shapes.	1. Written definitions, outlines of shapes with labels	1. All definitions included / Accurate shapes and labels
2. In groups of three, design a three dimensional building. This should be a building that could be built in your school or neighborhood. Include a scale in your design and show the land area as well as the size and shape of the building.	2. Scale drawing of building and land area with well defined dimensions	2. Drawing shows 3 dimensions / Land area and building use correct scale / Building is appropriate for land size and location
3. In the same group, construct a model based on your design.	3. Scale model	3. Model well constructed / Model follows design / Model built accurately to scale

Optional Student-Parent Cooperative Activity

Student Choices in Ways to Learn	Product/Performance Student Choice	Due Dates Student Choice Activities
Visual _____		
Verbal _____		
Kinesthetic _____		
Technological _____		

ACTIVITIES – STUDENT CHOICES

Visual	Verbal
1. Design the face of a building. Label 10 line segments and at least 3 other shapes. 2. Make an illustrated chart showing 3 dimensional shapes and their attributes.	5. Write a short story or poem that uses at least 10 geometric shape words. 6. Choose any picture of a city that has several buildings in it. Write a description of the picture using only geometric shape words to help you describe what you see.

Kinesthetic	Technological
3. Make and label 3-D models of 5 different shapes. 4. Make a collage of shapes that can be found in nature. Include labels with shape names in your collage.	7. Produce a 5 minute video showing the variety of shapes found in the "real world". Include both man-made and natural objects. 8. Do e-mail interviews with three different people who use their knowledge of shapes in their work. Include 8 or more questions in your interview. Write a summary of what you learn from these interviews.

Assessment of Student Choices – Geometric Shapes Individual Lesson Plan

1. Design of Building (Visual)
- Face of building is clearly drawn ___
- Has 10 line segments that are labeled ___
- Has 3 or more other shapes that are labeled ___

Suggested extension: Design several buildings with different shapes. ___

Possible points = ___

2. Illustrated Chart (Visual)
- Follows Chart criteria card ___
- Includes 5 different 3-dimensional shapes ___
- Attributes of each shape are stated clearly and accurately ___
- Illustrations are neat, accurately drawn and show each shape clearly ___

Possible points = ___

3. Models (Kinesthetic)
- Follows Model criteria card ___
- Has five 3-D models ___
- Each model is of a different shape ___
- Each shape is accurately labeled and spelled correctly ___

Possible points = ___

4. Collage (Kinesthetic)
- Follows Collage criteria card ___
- Shows 5 or more different shapes ___
- Each shape is from something in nature ___
- Each shape is accurately labeled and spelled correctly ___

Possible points = ___

5. Poem or Story (Verbal)
- Uses correct spelling, punctuation and grammar ___
- Uses 10 geometric shape words ___ **OR**
- Story has a beginning, middle and end ___
- Poem tells a story and/or describes something ___

Possible points = ___

6. Written Description (Verbal)
- Includes picture of several buildings ___
- Descriptions are clearly and accurately written ___
- Correct spelling, grammar and mechanics ___
- Uses at least 5 geometric shape words in descriptions ___

Possible points = ___

7. Video (Technological)
- Follows Video criteria card ___
- Video is 5 minutes long ___
- Shows 5 or more shapes & includes shape names for each ___

Suggested extension: Include original or unique elements.

Possible points = ___

8. E-mail Interviews & Summary (Technological)
- Three people interviewed ___
- All use knowledge of shapes in their work ___
- Interview has 8 or more questions ___
- Accurate, clear summary with good spelling, punctuation & grammar ___

Possible points = ___

Individual Lesson Plan – Math in History

Required Activities Teacher's Choice	Product/Performance Required	Assessment – Required Activities
1. Participate in class discussion of math history.	1. Notes from class discussion Any written work as required from teacher	1. All involved in discussion Notes or other written work complete and accurate
2. As a class, make a list of major mathematical discoveries that have impacted everyday life.	2. Class list	2. List has at least 10 major discoveries Individual quiz for knowledge and understanding of the topic

Optional Student-Parent Cooperative Activity

Student Choices in Ways to Learn	Product/Performance Student Choice	Due Dates Student Choice Activities
Visual _____		
Verbal _____		
Kinesthetic _____		
Technological _____		

ACTIVITIES – STUDENT CHOICES

Visual	Verbal
1. Make a time line of math history dating back to the Babylonians. Include at least 15 major mathematical discoveries.	5. Research a significant person or object in mathematical history. Teach a lesson to your class explaining the significance of this object or person.
2. Draw a diagram of an important mathematically based invention.	6. Write an explanation of the trigonometry involved in a sundial.

Kinesthetic	Technological
3. Make a model of an abacus labeling the parts. Write a short explanation of its history.	7. On the Internet, research a mathematical topic of your choice. Create a chart or diagram showing contradictory information you find.
4. Dress as a famous mathematician and create a tableaux showing his era in history and his work.	8. Do a Powerpoint presentation summarizing information about Einstein you find on any five different websites. Which website would you most recommend and why?

Assessment of Student Choices – Math in History Individual Lesson Plan

1. Time Line of Math History (Visual)
- Follows Time Line criteria card _____
- Includes fifteen or more discoveries _____
- Accuracy _____
- Writes about the significance of each discovery _____

Possible points = _____

2. Diagram (Visual)
- Follows Diagram criteria card _____
- Invention is important to mathematics _____
- Diagram is accurate and understandable _____
- Mathematical formulas and calculations are included _____

Possible points = _____

3. Model of Abacus (Kinesthetic)
- Follows Model criteria card _____
- Looks and functions like an abacus _____
- Parts are labeled _____
- Accurate and clear written explanation _____

Possible points = _____

4. Tableau (Kinesthetic)
- Follows Tableau criteria card _____
- Can see what he/she is famous for by looking at tableau _____
- Details of person's mathematical work are obvious _____
- Historical era is shown in tableau _____

Possible points = _____

5. Teach a Lesson (Verbal)
- Follows Oral Report criteria card _____
- Significance is clearly explained _____
- Interesting activities during lesson _____
- Easy to understand the topic _____

Possible points = _____

6. Written Explanation (Verbal)
- Explains what a sundial is and how it works _____
- Shows and explains the trigonometry involved in the sundial _____
- Accurate information _____
- Correct spelling, punctuation and grammar _____

Possible points = _____

7. Internet Research with Chart or Diagram (Technological)
- Evidence of search on three or more websites _____
- Clear visual _____
- Contradictory information is shown _____

Suggested extension: Write your own conclusions and reasons for them. _____

Possible points = _____

8. Powerpoint Presentation (Technological)
- Follows Powerpoint criteria card _____
- Five different websites are noted _____
- All websites have information about Einstein _____
- Has recommended website and reasons for recommending it _____

Possible points = _____

Individual Lesson Plan – Rocks and Minerals

ACTIVITIES – STUDENT CHOICES

Required Activities Teacher's Choice	Product/Performance Required	Assessment – Required Activities
1. Read the textbook about types of rocks and answer the questions.	1. Answers to questions	1. Accurate and complete
2. Complete labs on Igneous Rocks, Metamorphic Rocks and Sedimentary Rocks.	2. Lab write-up for each lab	2. All information completed correctly and written in lab report
3. Discuss what minerals are and list some common uses for minerals in every-day life.	3. Class list	3. All members of the class are participating and contributing to the list and the discussion

Optional Student-Parent Cooperative Activity

Student Choices in Ways to Learn	Product/Performance Student Choice	Due Dates Student Choice Activities
Visual _____		
Verbal _____		
Kinesthetic _____		
Technological _____		

Visual	Verbal
1. Develop a brochure illustrating the uses of rocks.	5. Write a 250 word essay describing a walk through a rocky area. Be sure to use the terms igneous, sedimentary and metamorphic.
2. Draw diagrams of eight different intrusive rock formations. Include dikes, magma, stock, laccolith, sill, lava plateau and batholith.	6. Write and perform a skit showing the rock cycle. Include props as needed.

Kinesthetic	Technological
3. Using the contour lines from a topographic map, build a three-dimensional model of a famous rock formation.	7. Create a 3-minute TV commercial telling about the important uses of minerals.
4. Make a board game about rocks and minerals.	8. Develop a slide show about some aspect of rocks or minerals using at least 10 digital photos you have taken. Include narration to explain each picture.

Assessment of Student Choices – Rocks and Minerals Individual Lesson Plan

1. Brochure (Visual)
- Follows Brochure criteria card ____
- Includes five or more uses ____
- Accuracy ____
- Each use is illustrated and explained in writing ____

Possible points = ____

2. Diagrams (Visual)
- Follows Diagram criteria card ____
- Has a diagram for each rock formation ____
- Diagrams are accurate and understandable ____
- Each rock formation is labeled ____

Possible points = ____

3. Model of Rock Formation (Kinesthetic)
- Follows Model criteria card ____
- Contour lines read and followed correctly ____
- Location of formation shown on map ____
- Accurate written explanation of what it is and why it's famous ____

Possible points = ____

4. Board Game (Kinesthetic)
- Follows Board Game criteria card ____
- Game questions/answers are clear and accurate ____
- Game has facts and concepts about rocks and minerals ____

Suggested extension: Play game with a classmate.

Possible points = ____

5. Essay (Verbal)
- Correct length ____
- Correct spelling, grammar and punctuation ____
- Includes igneous, sedimentary and metamorphic rocks ____
- Can picture what the writer is seeing through descriptive words ____

Possible points = ____

6. Skit (Verbal)
- Follows Skit criteria card ____
- Props help show various rocks in cycle ____
- Accurate information ____
- All parts of rock cycle are shown ____

Possible points = ____

7. TV Commercial (Technological)
- Follows Video criteria card ____
- Accurate information ____
- Commercial is three minutes long ____
- Uses correct terminology for various minerals ____

Possible points = ____

8. Slide Show (Technological)
- At least ten slides are included ____
- Narration goes with each slide ____
- Accurate information ____
- Narration is clear and understandable ____

Possible points = ____

Individual Lesson Plan – Space Exploration

Required Activities Teacher's Choice	Product/Performance Required	Assessment – Required Activities
1. Read a non-fiction book or portion of your textbook about space travel and exploration. 2. Read a science-fiction book about space travel and exploration. 3. As a whole class, discuss what everyone learned from these books. Make a list of facts and fantasy regarding space travel and exploration.	1. & 2. Make a Venn diagram comparing and contrasting the ideas in the fiction and non-fiction books. 3. Class list	1. & 2. Accuracy Thoroughness Similarities and differences clearly shown 3. Accurate and complete list All participate

Optional Student-Parent Cooperative Activity

Student Choices in Ways to Learn	Product/Performance Student Choice	Due Dates Student Choice Activities
Visual _____ Verbal _____ Kinesthetic _____ Technological _____		

© Carolyn Coil, www.carolyncoil.com

ACTIVITIES – STUDENT CHOICES

Visual	Verbal
1. Make a detailed diagram of a spacecraft that has been launched sometime in the past. It can be either a manned or unmanned vehicle. Label all major parts. 2. On a world map, identify and label launch sites and tracking stations around the world.	5. Research the progress of the International Space Station. Write a position paper in favor of or opposing it. 6. Write a short science fiction story about a trip to outer space. Be creative but incorporate factual material about space.

Kinesthetic	Technological
3. Dress as an astronaut or as a fictional space traveler. Present a skit showing at least five things that have to be done to prepare for space travel. 4. Make a diorama showing some aspect of space exploration.	7. Develop a 5-minute video promoting the development of a community on Mars. Include facts about Mars and what could be done to make this environment a place where humans could live. 8. Make a list of your ten favorite websites about space exploration. Write a short explanation about why each website is a good one.

96

© Pieces of Learning

Assessment of Student Choices – Space Exploration Individual Lesson Plan

1. Diagram (Visual)
- Labels are clear, correct and neatly written ___
- Accurate diagram of chosen spacecraft ___
- Neatly drawn and easily understood ___

Suggested extensions: Explain the functions of each part of the spacecraft. Write a report about the development and history of this spacecraft. ___

Possible points = ___

2. Map Identification (Visual)
- At least 10 locations labeled ___
- Locations are accurate ___
- Clear and neat with correct spelling ___

Suggested extension: Write an explanation about each location including its function in the space program. ___

Possible points = ___

3. Skit (Kinesthetic)
- Actions and words clearly show five things to prepare for space flight ___
- Details are accurate ___
- Gestures, facial expressions and props enhance message ___
- Costume appropriate and adds to information given in the skit ___

Possible points = ___

4. Diorama (Kinesthetic)
- Follows Diorama criteria card ___
- Clearly shows an aspect of space exploration ___
- Details are accurate ___

Suggested extension: Write an explanation of scene with resources listed. ___

Possible points = ___

5. Position Paper (Verbal)
- Your position on the International Space Station is clear ___
- Three or more reasons given for this position ___
- Reasons are supported by facts and examples ___
- Correct spelling, punctuation and grammar ___

Possible points = ___

6. Science Fiction Story (Verbal)
- Story has a beginning, middle and end ___
- Descriptions and settings include scientific facts ___
- Correct spelling, grammar and mechanics ___
- Creatively mixing fact with fiction in an interesting way ___

Possible points = ___

7. Video (Technological)
- Follows Video criteria card ___
- Video is 5 minutes long ___
- Gives accurate details and examples about Mars ___
- Includes creative yet feasible ideas about a Mars community ___

Possible points = ___

8. Favorite Websites (Technological)
- Lists 10 websites about space exploration ___
- Explanation conveys information well and tells why each is good ___
- Accurate information about each website ___

Suggested extension: Email questions to each website. Summarize responses to your questions. ___

Possible points = ___

Individual Lesson Plan – Study of a Novel

Required Activities Teacher's Choice	Product/Performance Required	Assessment – Required Activities
1. Read the novel assigned by your teacher. Participate in class discussion.	1. Contributions to class discussion	1. Informal observations during class discussion
2. Develop an outline for the novel. Include several literary elements.	2. Outline	2. Correct outline form. Five or more literary elements noted
3. Write a summary of the novel in correct essay form.	3. Essay	3. Structure & mechanics. Organization. Important parts of novel included in summary

Optional Student-Parent Cooperative Activity

Student Choices in Ways to Learn	Product/Performance Student Choice	Due Dates Student Choice Activities
Visual _____		
Verbal _____		
Kinesthetic _____		
Technological _____		

ACTIVITIES – STUDENT CHOICES

Visual	Verbal
1. Make a map showing the locations of important places in the story.	5. Write a poem showing your response to one of the characters or incidents in the novel.
2. Do a concept map or web showing traits of at least three characters.	6. Introduce a new character and write a different ending to the novel having this character play a major role.

Kinesthetic	Technological
3. Do a pantomime showing your favorite part of the story.	7. Do a PowerPoint presentation explaining the theme of the novel.
4. Create a dance that shows the plot of the novel. Include appropriate costumes.	8. Using the Internet, research the author of this novel. Present your findings in a product or performance of your choice.

Assessment of Student Choices – Study of a Novel Individual Lesson Plan

1. Map (Visual)

- Follows Map criteria card ____
- Accurate for story ____
- Has four or more locations clearly indicated ____

Suggested extension: Design a map to indicate something about plot or setting. ____

Possible points = ____

2. Concept Map or Web (Visual)

- Three characters clearly shown ____
- Several traits of each character are indicated ____
- Clear and neat with correct spelling ____

Suggested extension: Show how characters/traits interrelate with each other. ____

Possible points = ____

3. Pantomime (Kinesthetic)

- Actions clearly show portion of the story without using words ____
- Story details are accurate ____
- Gestures, facial expressions and props enhance message ____

Suggested extension: Include costumes and scenery. ____

Possible points = ____

4. Dance (Kinesthetic)

- Well-planned dance sequence ____
- Clearly shows main parts of novel ____
- Costumes help tell story ____
- Has appropriate music that shows the mood(s) of the novel ____

Possible points = ____

5. Poem (Verbal)

- Follows Poem criteria card ____
- Shows feelings and opinions about a character or incident ____
- Clearly relates to the novel ____

Suggested extension: Illustrate the poem. ____

Possible points = ____

6. Different ending (Verbal)

- New character is clearly described and interacts with existing characters ____
- Ending is feasible for the novel ____
- Correct spelling, grammar and mechanics ____

Suggested extension: Write an entire new chapter. ____

Possible points = ____

7. PowerPoint Presentation (Technological)

- Follows PowerPoint criteria card ____
- Theme is correctly identified ____
- Gives accurate details and examples about the theme ____

Suggested extension: Include original or unique elements in presentation. ____

Possible points = ____

8. Internet research (Technological)

- Uses three or more different websites ____
- Product/performance is interesting and conveys information well ____
- Accurate information about author ____

Suggested extension: Interview the author or publisher via email. Print the responses. ____

Possible points = ____

Individual Lesson Plan – Tobacco Use: Toward a Tobacco Free Society

ACTIVITIES – STUDENT CHOICES

Concrete Sequential	Concrete Random	Abstract Sequential	Abstract Random
1. Make a time line of the history of tobacco in the U. S. from the time of the early settlers to the present. 2. Figure out the cost of smoking for 1 year, 5 years, 10 years and 25 years. Construct a chart showing differences in cost depending upon how many cigarettes a person smokes each day.	5. Create an epitaph for an imaginary person. Include home, birth and death date along with a rhyming verse with an anti-tobacco message. 6. Make a poster for the school hall encouraging kids not to use tobacco.	3. Research the harmful effects of tobacco. Write a proposal banning smoking in any restaurant in the United States. Give at least three reasons along with facts to support your proposal. 4. Make a list of your five favorite websites that have a no smoking message. Write a paragraph about each and share this information with your class.	7. Write a short illustrated book for young children on why tobacco use is not good. Read this book to a kindergarten or first grade class. 8. Role play a scenario about tobacco use that has a positive ending. You will need others to participate in this role play.

Required Activities Teacher's Choice	Product/Performance Required	Assessment – Required Activities
1. Read articles about tobacco use. Outline main points and facts.	1. Outline	1. Accurate and complete Major points noted
2. Find an ad for tobacco in a magazine. Redesign the ad to show the real effects of tobacco.	2. Redesigned ad	2. Eye catching ad Effects of tobacco are evident
3. Write a letter to a smoker (real or imaginary) giving reasons why he or she should quit smoking.	3. Letter	3. Correct letter format At least three reasons given Well organized Correct grammar, spelling and punctuation

Optional Student-Parent Cooperative Activity

Student Choices in Ways to Learn	Product/Performance Student Choice	Due Dates Student Choice Activities
Concrete Sequential		
Abstract Sequential		
Concrete Random		
Abstract Random		

Assessment of Student Choices – Tobacco Use Individual Lesson Plan

1. Time Line (Concrete Sequential)

- Follows Time Line criteria card _____
- Includes ten or more items _____
- Accuracy _____
- Each item is related to tobacco _____

Possible points = _____

2. Chart (Concrete Sequential)

- Follows Chart criteria card _____
- Has data for 1, 5, 10 and 25 years _____
- Correct calculations _____

Possible points = _____

Suggested extension: Show how much money a non-smoker would save in an average lifetime. _____

3. Proposal (Abstract Sequential)

- Has facts about harmful effects of smoke and smoking _____
- Includes other facts to back up proposal _____
- Logical arguments with three or more reasons _____
- Correct spelling, grammar and mechanics _____

Possible points = _____

4. Website List (Abstract Sequential)

- Has a list of five websites _____
- Each website is summarized _____
- Correct paragraph form, grammar, spelling and mechanics _____

Possible points = _____

Suggested extension: Email website contacts with questions you have about tobacco use. Print your emails and responses. _____

5. Epitaph (Concrete Random)

- Looks like a tombstone _____
- Verse or message rhymes _____
- Message is anti-tobacco _____
- Has person's name, home, birth date and date of death _____

Possible points = _____

6. Poster (Concrete Random)

- Follows Poster criteria card _____
- Has anti-tobacco message _____
- Accurate information _____
- Uses persuasive language _____

Possible points = _____

7. Illustrated Book (Abstract Random)

- Follows Illustrated Book criteria card _____
- Accurate information _____
- Suitable for young children _____
- Reading to children is clear, fluent and with expression _____

Possible points = _____

8. Role Play (Abstract Random)

- Has a positive message about tobacco use _____
- Planning for role play is evident _____
- Accurate information _____
- Words are clear and understandable _____

Possible points = _____

Individual Lesson Plan – Winter Holidays

Required Activities Teacher's Choice	Product/Performance Required	Assessment – Required Activities
1. Read a book or short story about a winter holiday. This will be read by the whole class. Each student will take notes while reading.	1. Notes about book or story	1. Notes have major details and ideas from story. Notes are accurate and are done daily
2. Discuss characters, setting, theme and plot.	2. Class discussion	2. Participation
3. Make a 'Like and Different' chart showing which parts of the book are similar to your experiences and which are different.	3. 'Like and Different' chart	3. At least 3 items in each column. Clearly shows similarities and differences. Neat and readable chart

Optional Student-Parent Cooperative Activity

Student Choices in Ways to Learn	Product/Performance Student Choice	Due Dates Student Choice Activities
Visual _____ Verbal _____ Kinesthetic _____ Technological _____		

ACTIVITIES – STUDENT CHOICES

Visual	Verbal
1. Create a collage showing a number of different ways lights and candles are used in winter celebrations.	5. Write and perform a skit showing winter holiday customs in a culture other than your own.
2. Design a brochure comparing and contrasting four different types of holiday greenery: • Mistletoe • Holly • Evergreen trees • Wreaths	6. Write a story that contains traditional perceptions about Santa but also includes new ideas and adventures.

Kinesthetic	Technological
3. Cut designs in 10 paper bags and make a set of original and unique luminaries.	7. Develop a Power-Point presentation showing winter holiday celebrations in several different cultures.
4. Make a set of 7 clay or wooden figures that relate to the 7 principles of Kwanzaa.	8. Interview 5 people of different ages and from different cultures. Make an audio tape of their winter holiday memories.

102

Assessment of Student Choices - Winter Holidays Individual Lesson Plan

1. Collage (Visual)

- Follows Collage criteria card _____
- Includes at least 6 types of lights and candles _____
- Represents several different cultures _____

Suggested extension: Write an explanation of uses of lights. _____

Possible points = _____

2. Brochure (Visual)

- Follows Brochure criteria card _____
- Includes 4 different types of greenery _____
- Shows similarities and differences in the greenery _____

Suggested extension: Make a sales brochure to sell greens. Include persuasive language. _____

Possible points = _____

3. Luminaries (Kinesthetic)

- Different designs on each of the 10 bags _____
- Light or candle in each bag _____
- Creative, unique and neatly done _____

Suggested extension: Relate design directly to holiday season. _____

Possible points = _____

4. Set of Figures (Kinesthetic)

- Follows Model criteria card _____
- Each figure represents one principle of Kwanzaa _____
- Label next to each figure identifying each principle _____

Suggested extension: Write details about principles on label. _____

Possible points = _____

5. Skit (Verbal)

- Follows Skit criteria card _____
- Several customs shown in skit _____
- Costumes and props are authentic for culture _____
- Written script easy to follow and contains dialogue and stage directions _____

Suggested extension: Invite other classes or parents to the skit. _____

Possible points = _____

6. Story (Verbal)

- Story has beginning, middle and end _____
- Includes traditional and new ideas about Santa _____
- Correct spelling, grammar and mechanics _____

Suggested extension: Illustrate story to be shared with younger students. _____

Possible points = _____

7. PowerPoint Presentation (Technological)

- Follows PowerPoint criteria card _____
- Includes at least 4 different cultures _____
- Accurate details about celebration in each culture _____

Suggested extension: Use original or unique elements in presentation. _____

Possible points = _____

8. Audio Tape (Technological)

- Five people interviewed _____
- Includes people of different ages and cultures _____
- Tape is clear and includes memories of all five _____

Suggested extension: Create sound effects or music on tape. _____

Possible points = _____

Use the form on the next page or on the *Activities and Assessments CD* to guide you in following these steps.)

___1. Decide on a major theme or topic for the unit.

___2. Generate a unit rationale, a broad list of essential questions, objectives and outcomes which would include several subject areas, and the enduring understandings you hope will come out of the unit.

___3. Correlate unit objectives and outcomes with state standards in several subject areas.

___4. Brainstorm a list of possible unit activities.

___5. Classify each activity according to learning modalities, learning styles, Bloom's taxonomy or multiple intelligences.

___6. Decide which will be student choice activities and which will be required of all students.

___7. Include one independent activity in the activities required of all students. This will be the activity all students can work on while you are meeting with small groups of students and discussing their student choice activities.

___8. Use the *Teaching Tools* Individualized Lesson Plan forms to organize your unit activities. You will find blank forms to use on pages 106, 108, 110, 112, and 114. You can also find these forms on the *Activities and Assessments* CD.

___9. Write all student choice activities in consecutive numerical order for easy reference. This way, you can keep a record of which students have chosen which activity just by recording the number of the activity. (See forms on pages 82-83)

___10. Find or develop resources and materials needed for the unit.

___11. Develop assessments to assess unit objectives, outcomes and standards. A checklist format for assessing the student choice activities can be found on pages 107, 109, 111, 113, and 115. These forms can also be found on the *Activities and Assessments* CD. You could also develop complete rubrics, tests or quizzes, observation logs, charts and a host of other assessment instruments.

___12. Develop daily lesson plans based on your unit plan.

Notes:

© Pieces of Learning

Planning Form for an ILP Unit using the *Teaching Tools* Format

Topic or Theme_____

What do I want my students to know about this topic? What are the essential questions we want to answer? What are the Big Ideas?

- _____

- _____

- _____

- _____

What state standards are we working to meet?

- _____

- _____

- _____

- _____

Possible Student Activities	Product/Performance	LM/LS/Bloom/MI
1. _____	_____	_____
2. _____	_____	_____
3. _____	_____	_____
4. _____	_____	_____
5. _____	_____	_____
6. _____	_____	_____
7. _____	_____	_____
8. _____	_____	_____
9. _____	_____	_____
10. _____	_____	_____
11. _____	_____	_____

Individual Lesson Plan – Learning Modalities

Required Activities Teacher's Choice	Product/Performance Required	Assessment – Required Activities

Optional Student-Parent Cooperative Activity

Student Choices in Ways to Learn	Product/Performance Student Choice	Due Dates Student Choice Activities
Visual _____ Verbal _____ Kinesthetic _____ Technological _____		

© Carolyn Coil, www.carolyncoil.com

ACTIVITIES – STUDENT CHOICES

Visual	Verbal
Kinesthetic	**Technological**

Assessment of Student Choices - Individual Lesson Plan – Learning Modalities

1. _____ (Visual)

• • • •

Possible points = _____

2. _____ (Visual)

• • • •

Possible points = _____

3. _____ (Kinesthetic)

• • • •

Possible points = _____

4. _____ (Kinesthetic)

• • • •

Possible points = _____

5. _____ (Verbal)

• • • •

Possible points = _____

6. _____ (Verbal)

• • • •

Possible points = _____

7. _____ (Technological)

• • • •

Possible points = _____

8. _____ (Technological)

• • • •

Possible points = _____

Individual Lesson Plan – Learning Styles

Required Activities Teacher's Choice	Product/Performance Required	Assessment – Required Activities

Optional Student-Parent Cooperative Activity

Student Choices in Ways to Learn	Product/Performance Student Choice	Due Dates Student Choice Activities
Concrete Sequential _____ Abstract Sequential _____ Concrete Random _____ Abstract Random _____		

ACTIVITIES – STUDENT CHOICES

Concrete Sequential	Concrete Random

Abstract Sequential	Abstract Random

Assessment of Student Choices – Individual Lesson Plan – Learning Styles

1. _____ (Concrete Sequential)

• • • •

Possible points = ____

2. _____ (Concrete Sequential)

• • • •

Possible points = ____

3. _____ (Abstract Sequential)

• • • •

Possible points = ____

4. _____ (Abstract Sequential)

• • • •

Possible points = ____

5. _____ (Concrete Random)

• • • •

Possible points = ____

6. _____ (Concrete Random)

• • • •

Possible points = ____

7. _____ (Abstract Random)

• • • •

Possible points = ____

8. _____ (Abstract Random)

• • • •

Possible points = ____

Individual Lesson Plan – Taxonomy

Required Activities Teacher's Choice	Product/Performance Required	Assessment – Required Activities

Optional Student-Parent Cooperative Activity

Student Choices in Ways to Learn	Product/Performance Student Choice	Due Dates Student Choice Activities
Application ___		
Analysis ___		
Synthesis ___		
Evaluation ___		

ACTIVITIES – STUDENT CHOICES

Application	Synthesis
Analysis	Evaluation

Assessment of Student Choices – Individual Lesson Plan – Bloom's Taxonomy

1. _____ (Application)

• • • •

Possible points = _____

2. _____ (Application)

• • • •

Possible points = _____

3. _____ (Analysis)

• • • •

Possible points = _____

4. _____ (Analysis)

• • • •

Possible points = _____

5. _____ (Synthesis)

• • • •

Possible points = _____

6. _____ (Synthesis)

• • • •

Possible points = _____

7. _____ (Evaluation)

• • • •

Possible points = _____

8. _____ (Evaluation)

• • • •

Possible points = _____

Individual Lesson Plan – Multiple Intelligences

Required Activities Teacher's Choice	Product/Performance Required	Assessment – Required Activities

Optional Student-Parent Cooperative Activity

Student Choices in Ways to Learn	Product/Performance Student Choice	Due Dates Student Choice Activities
Verbal/Linguistic _____ Musical/Rhythmic _____ Logical/Mathematical _____ Visual/Spatial _____		

© Carolyn Coil, www.carolyncoil.com

ACTIVITIES – STUDENT CHOICES

Verbal/Linguistic	Musical/Rhythmic
	.

Logical/Mathematical	Visual/Spatial

© Pieces of Learning

Assessment of Student Choices - Individual Lesson Plan – Multiple Intelligences

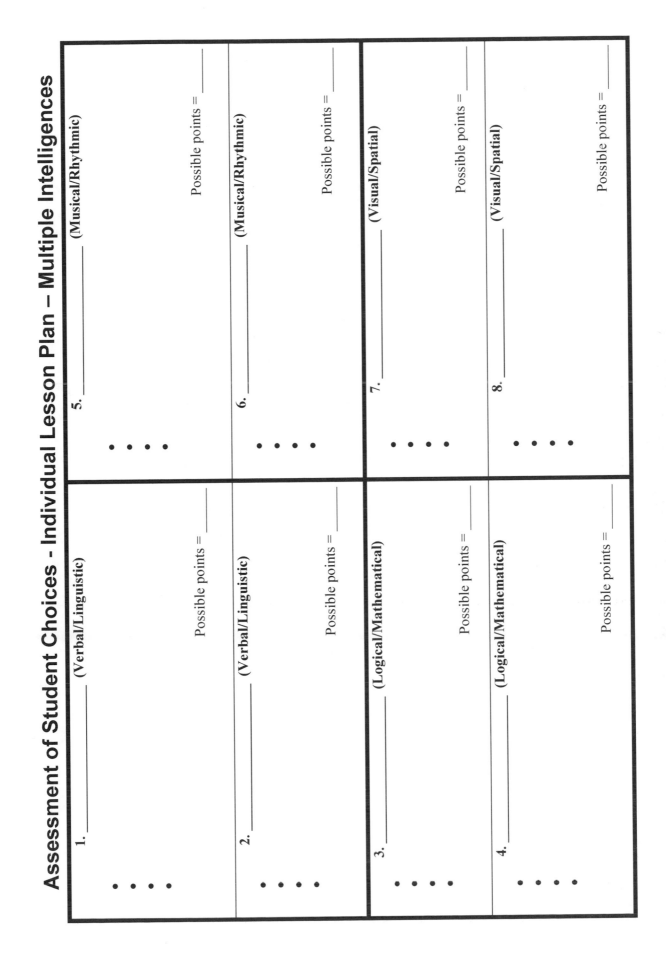

1. _____ (Verbal/Linguistic)

Possible points = _____

2. _____ (Verbal/Linguistic)

Possible points = _____

3. _____ (Logical/Mathematical)

Possible points = _____

4. _____ (Logical/Mathematical)

Possible points = _____

5. _____ (Musical/Rhythmic)

Possible points = _____

6. _____ (Musical/Rhythmic)

Possible points = _____

7. _____ (Visual/Spatial)

Possible points = _____

8. _____ (Visual/Spatial)

Possible points = _____

Individual Lesson Plan – Multiple Intelligences

Required Activities Teacher's Choice	Product/Performance Required	Assessment – Required Activities

Optional Student-Parent Cooperative Activity

Student Choices in Ways to Learn	Product/Performance Student Choice	Due Dates Student Choice Activities
Bodily/Kinesthetic _____ Intrapersonal _____ Naturalist _____ Interpersonal _____		

© Carolyn Coil, www.carolyncoil.com

ACTIVITIES – STUDENT CHOICES

Bodily/Kinesthetic	Naturalist
Intrapersonal	**Interpersonal**

Assessment of Student Choices - Individual Lesson Plan – Multiple Intelligences

1. _____ (Bodily/Kinesthetic)

• • • •

Possible points = _____

2. _____ (Bodily/Kinesthetic)

• • • •

Possible points = _____

3. _____ (Intrapersonal)

• • • •

Possible points = _____

4. _____ (Intrapersonal)

• • • •

Possible points = _____

5. _____ (Naturalist)

• • • •

Possible points = _____

6. _____ (Naturalist)

• • • •

Possible points = _____

7. _____ (Interpersonal)

• • • •

Possible points = _____

8. _____ (Interpersonal)

• • • •

Possible points = _____

Tiered Lessons and Units

What are Tiered Lessons and Units?

Tiered assignments provide for differentiation by allowing students of varying abilities or levels of readiness to work on the same basic content. Tiered lessons are best used with mixed-ability classes. They are an excellent way to provide diverse levels of activities for students, all of which are centered on the same key concepts, knowledge, standards or objectives. Since education is now intensely focused on all students working toward the standards, tiered lessons provide an excellent means for accomplishing this objective.

Tiered lessons encourage achievement in all students. Having different levels of activities promotes success in learning the standards without being too easy and boring for some or too difficult and anxiety-producing for others. In a typical "one-size-fits-all" classroom, students who see schoolwork as something that is almost always over their heads worry about being failures or not being able to successfully complete the assignment. Their brains shut down, and they may become defensive about why they won't do a certain task.

At the same time, students who view schoolwork as too easy can become unmotivated and often do not develop the work habits, organizational skills, and study skills they need. They become lazy thinkers, not because they are innately lazy, but because they don't need to engage much of their brains in order to do the work.

Tiering activities and assignments addresses the needs of both lower and higher-ability students and helps teachers target students at their individual levels of readiness. Learning is usually most successful when the required activity is just a bit more difficult than a student's comfort level. A good level (the level of readiness) is where a student understands what he or she is supposed to do but needs some help with the steps or the process for doing it. Tiered lessons provide a planning format for teachers for students of varying abilities.

The Tiered Lesson/Unit format includes both whole class activities and leveled activities. The whole class activities usually function to introduce a topic or to motivate and interest the entire class in a particular aspect of the subject. Guest speakers, audio-visual presentations, and many class discussions or hands-on activities are included.

The leveled activities are designed specifically to challenge students at their appropriate levels. Make all levels equally inviting and more or less parallel in terms of the type of activity and the amount of time it is likely to take.

There are 15 Tiered Lesson Plans in this section of the book. They include whole class activities and leveled activities plus assessment criteria for both. Use these as appropriate for your class, grade level, and subject. At the end of this section, you will find guidelines and blank forms for writing your own. They are also on the *Activities and Assessments* CD.

Two of the biggest concerns teachers have when using <u>Tiered Lessons</u> are how to put students into levels and how to grade leveled work. Neither of these questions have easy answers. Some suggestions for dealing with both of these issues are discussed below.

Establishing the Appropriate Level for Each Student

Identifying appropriate student levels can be done in several ways. Trial and error is probably the best strategy to use to find out what works best:

• Assign each student a level based on your own best judgment or on the basis of some type of pre-assessment. These assessments can be formal in nature, such as a pretest or standardized test score, or can be more informal such as observation of students or via a brainstorming activity, KWL chart (or other visual organizer) or class discussion.

• Give students a choice of 2 levels out of the 3. Place Level 1 and Level 2 activities on one sheet of paper (perhaps color coded) and Level 2 and Level 3 activities on another sheet of paper (in another color). Give some students one color and others the other color. In theory all students could choose Level 2, but with this limited choice most should pick their most appropriate level.

• Give your students an open choice. Teachers are hesitant to do this! However, many of your students may surprise you and choose their appropriate level. There are other students who invariably will choose the easiest learning activity, and there may be a few who will choose a level of inappropriate difficulty. You may want to reserve the right to veto a student's choice. This may be something you want to try after you have assigned several tiered lessons.

Grading Tiered Assignments

Grading tiered assignments often produces the most concern when teachers decide to implement this strategy. Below are some possible ways to handle the grading dilemma:

1. Have activities at all levels equal the same number of points. The reason is that if each student is working at his/her appropriate level, he/she should be graded according to how well he/she has done at that level and not compared to other students. This is particularly appropriate for formative assessments and less appropriate for summative assessments where students are generally compared to one another.

2. Give more points to students who attempt the higher level tasks. For example, a Level 1 activity might be worth a total of 85 points while a Level 3 activity might be worth 100 points.

3. Decide which level represents grade level work and have that level worth 100 points. Students working at a lower level would receive less points and those working at a higher level could receive bonus or additional points.

Tiered Lesson Plan: Animals

Objectives or Standards

1. Students will compare and describe different animals in the ways they look, grow and move.
2. Students will know the six animal classifications.
3. Students will compare and contrast various animal groups.
4. Each student will become a class expert on one animal.

Whole Class Activities

1. Students will brainstorm a list of all the animals they can think of. Teacher will record the list on chart paper.
2. In three heterogeneous groups, students will list as many ways as they can think of that animals move (group 1), look (group 2) and grow (group 3). Groups will share what they have discussed.
3. Teacher will introduce the six major classifications of animals: insects, fish, birds, amphibians, reptiles, and mammals.
4. Characteristics of each type of animal will be learned through a story, text readings or video.
5. Students will classify the class animal list according to the six animal groups.

Assessment

❑ All listening, participating and asking questions in both the large group and small groups as appropriate.

Level 1 Activities

1. Each student will choose one animal classification and make a flipbook featuring ten animals in that classification. The flipbook will have a picture of each animal and at least one unique characteristic about the animal.

2. Each student will invent an imaginary animal that could be in that classification and add it to his or her flipbook with a picture and description.

3. Each student will choose one animal from this classification and write a one-page report on it.

Assessment

☞ ❑ All animals in the flipbook are from the chosen classification.
❑ Includes ten animals with picture and one or more characteristics.

☞ ❑ Imaginary animal has correct characteristics for classification.
❑ Description and picture go together.

❑ Report is at least one page long.
☞ ❑ Has facts about one animal in the chosen classification.
❑ Is accurate.
❑ Has correct spelling, grammar and punctuation.

Level 2 Activities

1. Each student will choose two different animal classifications and make a Venn diagram comparing and contrasting them.

2. Each student will invent an imaginary animal combining the characteristics of the two animal groups. Each student will draw a picture of his or her imaginary animal and write a description of the animal including how the animal would eat, grow and move.

3. Each student will choose a real animal from one of the two groups and write a two-page paper about that animal.

Assessment

❏Has two different animal classifications.
❏Clearly shows similarities and differences.

❏Imaginary animal combines characteristics.
❏Picture is neatly done.
❏Detailed.
❏Goes with description.
❏Explains how animal eats, moves and grows.

❏Report is at least two pages long.
❏Has facts about one animal in the chosen classification.
❏Is accurate.
❏Has correct spelling, grammar and punctuation.

Level 3 Activities

1. Each student will list the advantages and disadvantages of characteristics of each of the six classifications of animals. There should be at least 3 advantages and 3 disadvantages for each classification.

2. Each student will invent an imaginary animal combining the characteristics of three animal groups. Each student will draw a picture of his or her imaginary animal and write a description of the animal including how the animal would eat, grow and move.

3. Each student will choose an animal that does not easily fit into one classification and write a two-page report, including details about how to classify the animal.

Assessment

❏List includes all six classifications clearly showing 3 advantages and 3 disadvantages of each.

❏Imaginary animal combines characteristics of three groups.
❏Picture is neatly done.
❏Detailed.
❏Goes with description.
❏Explains how animal eats, moves and grows.

❏Report is at least two pages long. ❏Has facts about one animal that does not easily fit into a classification. ❏Is accurate. ❏Has correct spelling, grammar and punctuation.

Whole Class Culminating Activities

1. Students will work in heterogeneous groups sharing their pictures and descriptions.

2. Students will participate in a game of animal classification in a BINGO format with the teacher calling out characteristics and students marking BINGO cards filled with animals.

Assessment

❏Group participation.
❏Ability to read own writing.
❏Clear presentation.
❏Ability to listen to others.

❏Correct identification of animals with five correct answers in a BINGO format.

Tiered Lesson Plan: Compound Words

Objectives or Standards

1. Students will recognize the structure of compound words.
2. Students will understand how and when compound words are used.
3. Students will create and use compound words.

Whole Class Activities

1. Demonstrate how compound words are created by using puzzle pieces with simple words to make compound words.

2. Listen to and sing the "Grammar Rock" song on compound words.

Assessment

❑All look and listen to teacher's demonstration.

❑All students singing and participating.

Level 1 Activities

1. Have these students make their own compound words from the puzzle pieces and write them on a sheet of paper.

2. Write 10 sentences using these compound words.

Assessment

❑All words created are compound words.

❑Correct spelling of words.
❑All words used.
❑Has 10 sentences.

Level 2 Activities

1. Generate a list of 10 new compound words. Highlight each part of the compound word with a different color.

2. Write two paragraphs using all 10 words.

Assessment

❑Has 10 compound words.
❑Parts are indicated correctly.

❑Paragraphs are in correct form with main idea.
❑All 10 words used.

120

Level 3 Activities

1. Make a dictionary with 10 original compound words. Define and illustrate each.

2. Write a short story using these 10 words.

Assessment

☞ ❑Has 10 original words and definitions.
❑Words are illustrated.
❑In alphabetical order.

☞ ❑Story uses all 10 words.
❑Has a plot with a beginning, middle and end.

Whole Class Culminating Activities

1. Share products from Levels 1, 2 and 3.

2. "Walking Words" activity where each student holds a word and finds a partner to make a compound word.

Assessment

❑Group participation

Tiered Lesson Plan: Early Explorations

Objectives or Standards

1. Learn some of the stories about the first European visits to America.
2. Understand the role of the Vikings in early explorations.
3. Compare and contrast early maps to our maps of today.
4. Relate events of the past in making implications for the past.

Whole Class Activities

1. On a piece of plain white paper, have each student draw a map of the world from memory. They should include continents, oceans and any other details they can remember.

2. Put students in pairs to compare and contrast their maps, making a list of similarities and differences. Then they are to look at an actual world map and identify things on their maps that are correct and things that are incorrect.

3. Discuss what the students learned from this activity. What conclusions can they make about early mapmakers?

Assessment

☞ ❑All participate in map drawing.

☞ ❑List has both similarities and differences.
❑Incorrect details identified.

☞ ❑All participate.
❑Class conclusions recorded.

Level 1 Activities

1. Use your textbook or other reference materials to find a drawing or diagram of a Viking ship. List 5 ideas you have about their voyages from looking at the ship.

2. Find out about the voyages of Leif Eriksson. Pretend you are a member of the crew on one of his ships. Write a letter home telling about the ship, your journey, and all the things you are seeing as you travel.

Assessment

☞ ❑Lists 5 or more ideas.
❑Ideas are reasonable.
❑Conclusions based on reference information.

☞ ❑Historically correct details.
❑Correct letter format.
❑Correct spelling, grammar and punctuation.
❑Show appropriate point of view

Level 2 Activities

1. Compare and contrast a globe used at the time of the early explorers (such as Behaim's globe) with a globe of today. Use a chart to record similarities and differences.

☞ ❑Similarities and differences clearly shown on chart.
❑Accurate information.

2. Find out about Muslim maps of the 700s and the maps the Vikings used. Draw maps of the world from these two perspectives.

☞ ❑Two clearly drawn maps.
❑Correct details for each map.

Level 3 Activities

Assessment

Create a newspaper with:
1. A story describing the attack on Thorvald and the Vikings in Vinland.

☞ ❑Accurate descriptions and details.

2. An opinion column about exploration from the point of view of a European who doesn't want to continue explorations.

☞ ❑Opinions clearly stated.
❑Several reasons given for each opinion.
❑Includes maps to illustrate point of view.
❑Historically accurate details.

3. An opinion column from the point of view of a Viking who encourages exploration by telling about Viking successes in many parts of the world.

☞ ❑Two clearly drawn maps.
❑Correct details for each map

Whole Class Culminating Activities

Assessment

1. Share products from leveled activities.

☞ ❑Informal observation.

2. In a TV talk show format, interview one person from each level. All students can ask questions about information learned at each level. Others who worked at the same level can assist the person being interviewed in answering the questions.

☞ ❑Questions are relevant.
❑Information and answers are accurate.
❑Cooperative attitude among all students.

3. Group students heterogeneously with representatives from each of the levels in each group. Ask them to discuss and make a list of things we can learn from early explorations that apply to our lives today.

☞ ❑Lists are reasonable and relevant to the topic.
❑Each list has 3 or more ideas.

Tiered Lesson Plan: Fractions, Decimals & Percents

Objectives or Standards

1. Students will comprehend the relationship between fractions, decimals and percents.
2. Students will be able to change fractions to decimals to percents and vice-versa.
3. Students will understand how fractions, decimals and percents are used in the real world.

Whole Class Activities

1. Teacher will introduce the concept that fractions, decimals and percents are interrelated. In a whole class discussion, students and the teacher will generate several examples.

2. The teacher will demonstrate the process of changing fractions to decimals and decimals to percents.

3. Students will practice this process by completing assigned worksheet or page(s) from math book. Students can take test for mastery.

Assessment

❑All listening and participating

❑Traditional grading on worksheets, pages from book and/or test.

Level 1 Activities

1. Create a poster with a diagram showing the steps for changing fractions to decimals to percents and vice-versa.

2. Create a survey where the answers will be given in the form of fractions.

Assessment

☞ ❑Accurate diagram showing five or more steps.
❑Follows Poster criteria card.

☞ ❑Survey has at least five questions.
❑All questions have options written in fraction form.

124

Level 2 Activities

1. Using a list of given ratio relationships, write a newspaper article reporting the information using the appropriate fraction, decimal or percent equivalents.

☞ ❑Accurate information.
❑Accurate mathematical calculations.
❑Appropriate topic for class.

2. Create a survey that combines decimals and percents in the answers. Include the same or similar questions with the answers written in different ways.

☞ ❑Survey has at least 10 questions.
❑Some questions are similar.
❑There is a mix of decimals and percents in the answers.

Level 3 Activities

Assessment

1. Write and solve three word problems that incorporate real world situations using fractions, decimals and percents.

☞ ❑Has three word problems.
❑Accurate solutions for each.
❑Problems have real world connection.

2. Create a survey that combines decimals, fractions and percents in the answers.

☞ ❑Survey has at least 10 questions.
❑Answers are a mix of fractions, decimals and percents.

Whole Class Culminating Activities

Assessment

1. Each student will give his/her survey to at least five different people.

☞ ❑Evidence that survey was given to five or more people.

2. Each student will make conclusions based on the information gotten from the survey.

☞ ❑Logical conclusions based on survey.

3. Students will share survey results and conclusions in groups of four.

☞ ❑Group cooperation and task commitment.

Tiered Lesson Plan: Graphs and Data

Objectives or Standards

1. Develop creativity and higher level thinking skills.
2. Collect and organize appropriate data.
3. Construct an accurate graph.
4. Analyze and interpret graphs.

Whole Class Activities

1. Brainstorm various ways one can collect and organize data. List on board or overhead.

2. Review parts of a graph. Demonstrate and illustrate different types of graphs and remind students how to construct different types of graphs.

3. Discuss the concept of "pleasing to the eye". Give examples and have students give or show examples from past assignments or their own classroom work.

4. Give Level 1 students homework to practice basic skills constructing graphs while Level 2 & 3 students gather data for their activities.

Assessment

☞ ❑All participate in class discussion.

☞ ❑All students listening and answering questions as needed.

☞ ❑Class conclusions recorded on a "Pleasing to the Eye" poster or criteria card.

☞ ❑Level 1: Shows accuracy in graphing skills.
❑Levels 2 & 3: Gather data accurately.

Level 1 Activities (Choose one)

1. Select a set of data already collected by the teacher. Organize the data. Construct a bar graph showing this data. Write five questions that could be answered by looking at your graph. Mount all materials on a 12"x18" sheet of construction paper.

2. Use statistics found in your social studies or science book to create a line graph. Organize the data. Write five questions that could be answered by looking at your graph. Mount all materials on a 12"x18" sheet of construction paper.

Assessment for Both

❑Follows Graph criteria card.

❑Five appropriate, well-constructed questions.

❑Correct spelling, punctuation and grammar.

❑Data shown accurately.

❑Visual is correct size.

❑Is pleasing to the eye.

Level 2 Activities (Choose one)

1. Choose a teacher-approved survey question. Conduct a survey gathering data from at least 25 different people. Organize the data. Construct a line or bar graph to show survey results. Explain results in a paragraph showing inferences and conclusions. Mount all materials on a 12"x18" sheet of construction paper.

☞ ❑Data gathered accurately from 25 or more people.

2. Gather two sets of weather statistics from newspapers, TV or the Internet. Organize this data and compare by constructing a double bar graph. Explain results in a paragraph drawing inferences and conclusions. Mount all materials on a 12"x18" sheet of construction paper.

☞ ❑Has two sets of weather statistics from different sources.
(Both)
❑Follows Graph criteria card.
❑Paragraph shows inferences and conclusions.
❑Has correct spelling, grammar and punctuation.
❑Visual is correct size.
❑Is pleasing to the eye.

Level 3 Activities (Choose one)

Assessment

1. Use percentage statistics found on the Internet, in a newspaper, magazine or almanac to answer a question or support a main idea. Organize the data and show on a circle graph. Explain results in a 7-10 sentence paragraph analyzing the results drawing inferences and conclusions. Mount all materials on a 12"x18" sheet of construction paper.

☞ ❑Shows question.
❑Shows resources.
❑Shows statistics.

2. Choose a teacher-approved survey question. Conduct a survey gathering data from 100 different people. Organize the data turning the statistics into percentages. Construct a circle graph to show survey results. Explain results in a 7-10 sentence paragraph analyzing results and drawing inferences and conclusions. Mount all materials on a 12"x18" sheet of construction paper.

☞ ❑Data gathered from 100 people.
❑Percentages are accurate and reflect the data gathered.
(Both)
❑Follows Graph criteria card.
❑Has 7-10 sentence paragraph with correct spelling, grammar and punctuation.
❑Correctly analyzes data and shows inferences and conclusions.
❑Visual is correct size and is pleasing to the eye.

Whole Class Culminating Activities

Assessment

Share products from Levels 1, 2 and 3.

❑Group participation

Objectives or Standards

1. To analyze literary characters.
2. To identify typical elements of life at a given time in history.
3. To understand how time period and setting affect literature.
4. Compare and contrast characters in literature.

Whole Class Activities

1. Discuss background information on a particular period in history.

2. Review literary elements of setting, plot, theme, characterization, conflict and climax. Discuss how an historical time period might affect these.

3. Read a short story or novel set in a particular time period in history. All students may read the same story or novel or they may read different ones at their appropriate reading level as directed by the teacher.

Assessment

❏ All participate in class discussion.

❏ All students read assigned book or story.

❏ All students take notes on characters, setting, plot and theme.

Level 1 Activities

1. Make a list of at least 5 characters in the story. Write a description of each, making sure to include both physical appearance and character traits.

2. Create an illustration of at least 2 characters in the historical setting from the book.

3. Compare and contrast these 2 characters using a Venn diagram.

Assessment

☞ ❏ List has 5 characters.
❏ Physical/emotional descriptions of each.
❏ Correct spelling, grammar, punctuation.

☞ ❏ Historically accurate.
❏ Clearly shows two characters.

☞ ❏ Similarities and differences distinctly shown on Venn diagram.
❏ Neat.
❏ Correct spelling.

Level 2 Activities

Level 2 Activities	**Assessment**

1. Make a chart listing 5 characters with information under these headings: <u>Problems Faced</u>; <u>Conflicts</u>; <u>How Historical Events Impacted</u>; <u>Relationships to Others</u>; <u>Other</u>.

☞ ❏Chart lists 5 characters.
❏Has required information.
❏Information is accurate.

2. Write a three-page paper analyzing these characters using the information from your chart.

☞ ❏Paper is three pages.
❏Shows relationships between the characters and events that affect them.
❏Has correct spelling, grammar and punctuation.

3. Design a visual showing similarities and differences between the characters.

☞ ❏Visual is clear.
❏Accurately shows similarities/differences.

Level 3 Activities	**Assessment**

1. Research the historical time period reflected in the book or story. List at least 10 new facts or ideas you learn that are not included in the story. Include 3 or more references.

☞ ❏Facts are accurate.
❏Based on correct time period.
❏Has 3 or more references written in a bibliography.

2. Analyze 5 characters in the book considering this new information. Using at least two incidents that happened to each character, explain why you think these are probable, possible or impossible based on your research. Defend your position using charts, graphs or diagrams and a written position paper.

☞ ❏Has graphic or visual that shows or justifies position.
❏Position paper states opinion clearly.
❏Is defended with appropriate facts.
❏Has correct spelling, grammar and punctuation.

Whole Class Culminating Activities	**Assessment**

1. Discussion of new knowledge about characters and the historical time period learned while doing Levels 1, 2 and 3.

☞ ❏Group participation.

2. Show video of another story in the same historical time period.

☞ ❏All watch and discuss afterwards.

Tiered Lesson Plan: Infectious Diseases

Objectives or Standards

1. Students will understand basic information about a variety of infectious diseases.
2. Students will see how infectious diseases can affect them and others around them.
3. Students will understand how infectious diseases are spread and how they can be prevented, treated and cured.
4. Each student will examine one infectious disease in depth.

Whole Class Activities

1. Read text, magazine articles and books, or search Internet sites for basic information about infectious diseases. Make a class list of all the infectious diseases you can find.

2. Each student will find out how one infectious disease has affected someone he or she knows and will write from 2-5 paragraphs about that disease, how the person was affected, types of treatment, and the results of treatment. For privacy reasons, this person does not need to be named.

3. Discuss the difference between an infectious disease and other types of diseases.

Assessment

❏General class discussion about the diseases on the class list.
❏Quiz identifying major infectious diseases.

❏Accuracy of information.
❏Includes effects of the disease, treatments and results.
❏Good sentence structure, grammar, mechanics and spelling.

❏All are listening and participating.

Level 1 Activities

1. Choose one disease. Draw a diagram showing how it begins and goes through the body. Label the disease and important parts of the diagram.

2. List three ways this disease could be prevented.

Assessment

❏Accurate diagram.
❏Correctly spelled labels.
❏Neatly and clearly drawn.

❏List has three items.
❏All items are accurate ways to prevent this disease.

Level 2 Activities

1. Choose a disease that worsens without proper treatment. Make a chart showing the stages of the disease.

❏Accurate information on chart.
❏Stages are clearly indicated.
❏Follows Chart criteria card.

2. Make a brochure for the prevention of this disease.

❏Follows Brochure criteria card.
❏Brochure has clear and feasible steps for disease prevention.

Level 3 Activities

Assessment

1. Make a web or concept map showing several interrelated infectious diseases.

❏Has three or more diseases.
❏Visual shows how diseases are interrelated.

2. Make a 3-column chart to show causes, symptoms and treatments for each. Use arrows or other visual indicators to show connections.

❏Chart shows causes, symptoms and treatments for each disease.
❏Connections are clearly shown.
❏Follows Chart criteria card.

Whole Class Culminating Activities

Assessment

1. Put students in groups of four with each group having representatives from each level.

❏Group cooperation, sharing and planning.

2. Share products from leveled activities.

3. Do a group role play for the class showing what you have learned about infectious diseases.

❏Role play clearly shows information about a variety of diseases.

4. Each student will make a personal plan of action for preventing infectious diseases.

❏All group members participate.

Tiered Lesson Plan: Informative Speech

Objectives or Standards

1. Students will examine coherent presentations that convey ideas clearly.
2. Students will deliver an informative speech with purpose and organization.
3. Students will use appropriate gestures and facial expressions and will have audible and clear speech, good eye contact, and good posture.
4. Students will use an appropriate visual aid in their speeches.

Whole Class Activities

1. Teacher will explain what an informative speech is and will review the elements found in an informative speech.

2. Students will view a video of a former student or an adult delivering an informative speech incorrectly.

3. Students will view a video of a former student or an adult delivering an informative speech correctly.

4. Discuss each video and list elements of a good and a poor informative speech.

5. Create a class rubric for an informative speech based on class ideas.

Level 1 Activities

1. Working in pairs, describe and define at least five elements of a good informative speech.

2. Select a topic. Working together, outline this topic according to the five elements.

3. Create a visual aid to go along with the topic.

4. Practice giving the speech to one another, being aware of the elements of a good speech. Use class rubric to critique one another in a helpful way.

Assessment

❑All listening and participating.

❑All students will take notes on what they observe in both videos.

❑All participate.
❑Class conclusions recorded.

❑Class rubric includes purpose, organization, gestures, facial expressions, audible speech, good posture and eye contact.

Assessment

☞ ❑Accurate list of five or more elements.

☞ ❑Outline includes elements defined above.
❑Topic is appropriate for an informative speech.

☞ ❑Visual is clear.
❑Easy to see.
❑Easy to understand.
❑Helps explain topic.

☞ ❑Peer evaluation.
❑Comments on rubric.

Level 2 Activities

<table>
<tr><td>

1. Choose a topic appropriate for an informative speech. This should be a topic you already know something about.

</td><td>

☞

</td><td>

❑Accurate information.
❑Appropriate topic for class.

</td></tr>
<tr><td>

2. Using the class rubric as a guide, prepare an informative speech to deliver to the class.

</td><td>

☞

</td><td>

❑Speech follows guidelines in class rubric.

</td></tr>
<tr><td>

3. Create a visual aid to go along with the speech.

</td><td>

☞

</td><td>

❑Visual is clear.
❑Easy to see.
❑Easy to understand.
❑Helps explain topic.

</td></tr>
</table>

Level 3 Activities

Assessment

<table>
<tr><td>

1. Pick a topic that requires a thesis statement and research to support your thesis.

</td><td>

☞

</td><td>

❑Appropriate topic.
❑Appropriate thesis statement.
❑Topic approved by teacher.

</td></tr>
<tr><td>

2. Use at least three sources to find information on your topic.

</td><td>

☞

</td><td>

❑At least 3 sources listed.
❑Correct bibliographical form.

</td></tr>
<tr><td>

3. Using the class rubric as a guide, prepare an informative speech to deliver to the class.

</td><td>

☞

</td><td>

❑Speech follows guidelines in class rubric.

</td></tr>
<tr><td>

4. Create a visual aid to go along with the speech.

</td><td>

☞

</td><td>

❑Visual is clear.
❑Easy to see.
❑Easy to understand.
❑Helps explain topic.

</td></tr>
</table>

Whole Class Culminating Activities

Assessment

<table>
<tr><td>

1. Each student will present his/her informative speech.

</td><td>

☞

</td><td>

❑Class rubric based on: purpose, organization, gestures, facial expressions, audible speech, good posture and eye contact.

</td></tr>
<tr><td>

2. Visual aid will be included in each speech.

</td><td>

☞

</td><td>

❑Visual is clear.
❑Easy to see.
❑Easy to understand.
❑Helps explain topic.

</td></tr>
</table>

Tiered Lesson Plan: Landforms

Objectives or Standards

1. Distinguish between city, suburban, small town and farm settings.
2. Identify various landforms and bodies of water.
3. Compare and contrast the physical features of the land.

Whole Class Activities

1. Discuss city, suburb, small town and farms. Find out who has lived in each of these.

2. Divide into heterogeneous groups. Assign each group one of the four areas listed above. Each group will make a chart listing information about their area.

3. Share charts, comparing and contrasting them.

Assessment

☞ ❑All participating in discussion.

☞ ❑Chart has 10 or more details.
❑Details are accurate for area assigned.

☞ ❑Accurate comparisons.

Level 1 Activities

1. Using a dictionary or glossary, write the definitions of these words: mountain, valley, plain, desert, river, lake, ocean, island. Illustrate each word.

2. Color an outline map of the United States showing mountains, plains and deserts each in a different color. Indicate which color is for which landform. Add oceans and lakes if desired.

Assessment

☞ ❑All 8 words defined correctly.
❑Pictures show meanings of words.

☞ ❑Landforms shown accurately on map.
❑Color representations indicated on map key.

Level 2 Activities

1. Create an illustrated dictionary using 20 words that name or describe the earth's physical features. Choose the words from your book or from any other reference.

2. Write a paragraph using as many of these words as possible.

Assessment

☞ ❑Words are alphabetized.
❑Pictures show meaning of words.
❑Accurate definitions.

☞ ❑Good sentence structure.
❑Has a main idea.
❑Uses at least 10 words.

Level 3 Activities

1. Give students a copy of the *Landforms Poems* by Nancy Polette. Working in pairs with a visual organizer, students will read the poems, then write and define descriptive nouns and adjectives that refer to the landform for each poem. Six words are underlined in each poem. Challenge students to find additional words.

☞ ❑Defines 6 or more words in each poem.
❑Detailed definitions.

2. In pairs, students will write their own poem using descriptive words about oceans, lakes or rivers.

☞ ❑Uses at least 6 descriptive words.
❑Verse is at least 6 lines long.

Whole Class Culminating Activities

Assessment

1. Give all students copies of the *Landforms Poems.* Read aloud together. With the help of Level 3 students, identify and define unknown words.

☞ ❑All participate.
❑Words are identified.
❑Words are defined through the discussion.

2. Share products from leveled activities.

☞ ❑Informal observation.

3. Discuss and do a web making connections between the physical features and man-made features of the earth.

☞ ❑Web shows several accurate connections.

LANDFORMS POEMS   by Nancy Polette

A Lowlands Supermarket

Take a shopping cart and dare to park it,
In a lowlands supermarket.
A buffalo on vast rolling <u>plains</u>,
The dinner table of the open range.

Small creatures shop in dell and glen,
Sampling nature's bounty then.
<u>Swamps</u> and marshes, dark murky water,
A food basket for the crocodile's daughter.

A <u>bayou</u>, a <u>gully</u>, a <u>bog</u> in the ground,
Food for the gator, dinner in the round.
In the <u>veld</u> and savannah, aisle after aisle,
of delicacies make an elephant smile.

When the food cart is full, dinner at nine,
In a secluded ravine, a safe place to dine.

A Mountain Guide

Guide would like to have a dime,
For every unsuccessful climb,
Up mountain slope and jagged <u>peak</u>,
By those the <u>pinnacle</u> to seek.

Beginners he has tried to teach,
The <u>summit</u> here is out of reach.
Guide thinks that he would like to change,
The Rockies to another <u>range</u>.

But what goes up, must come down,
(the <u>canyon</u>'s lower than the ground).
Guide waits beneath snow-covered <u>dome</u>,
When climbers choose to head for home.

But a climber's unsuccessful trip
Means guide will not receive a tip!

A Highland Fling

Don tartans and kilts, bring shield and lance,
The <u>tableland</u> sets the stage for dance.
The flat <u>mesa</u> serves for the Highland Reel,
Quick footwork, tap the toe and heel.

Behind a curtain of rolling hills,
Warrior chiefs enact bold kills.
To the Highland Fling with bagpipe sound,
Played by a pipe on <u>knoll</u> or mound.

Cold winds blow from <u>butte</u> and <u>cliff</u>,
Dancers' legs grow cold and stiff.
Whirling frenzy, sometimes rough,
Tradition honored from hill to <u>bluff</u>.

Tableland, mesa, knoll all sing,
The music of the Highland Fling.

A Desert Spa

An <u>oasis</u> massages the burning sands,
A cleansing facial for <u>barren</u> lands.
A body wrap for wind-swept <u>dunes</u>,
Aromatherapy to coyote tunes.

A <u>mirage</u> perhaps, on an <u>arid</u> face,
An <u>arroyo</u> usurps the oasis' place.

Descriptive
Words

A Lowlands Supermarket *(Lowlands)*	**A Highland Fling** *(Highlands)*
A Mountain Guide *(Mountains)*	**A Desert Spa** *(Desert)*

New Verse about _____

Tiered Lesson Plan: Map Skills

Objectives or Standards

1. Students will be able to explain the purpose of a map scale.
2. Students will be able to calculate the distance between points using a map scale.
3. Students will be able to use cardinal and intermediate directions on a map or globe.
4. Students will be able to use a map key to interpret symbols and read a map.
5. Students will be able to draw their own maps.

Whole Class Activities

1. Class will brainstorm all the different ways they have seen maps being used. Uses will be listed on board or chart paper.

2. Teacher will show students various kinds of maps. Each student will identify different elements on a map such as scale, key, compass rose, lines of latitude and longitude, cities, landforms, etc.

3. Teacher will explain how to use a map scale and how to measure distances from point to point on a map. In heterogeneous groups of 4, students will figure out distances between various points on a state, USA or world map.

Assessment

☞ ❑All students involved in brainstorming.
❑Involved in discussion.
❑List should have 10 or more examples.

☞ ❑Required items identified correctly.
❑All items are included.

☞ ❑Everyone in the group is participating.
❑All required distances are calculated correctly.
❑Students can explain how they figured out their answers.

Level 1 Activities

1. Students will work in pairs. Each pair will be given a state road map and will be given a list of 8-10 major cities. Using the map scale, they will figure distances between each major city and highlight the shortest route to go from one city to another.

2. Each student will make a grid map of the classroom including a scale and a key with symbols.

Assessment

☞ ❑Accurately identifies each city.
❑Distances calculated correctly.
❑Route between cities is the shortest way to go.

☞ ❑Map is neatly drawn.
❑Scale is correct.
❑Key uses three or more symbols.

138

Level 2 Activities

1. Students will work in pairs. Each pair will be given a state road map and will be given a list of 15 cities, small towns and tourist areas. Using the map scale, they will figure distances between each place and highlight two logical routes to go from one place to another for all 15 locations.
2. Each student will make a grid map of their neighborhood, including a scale and a key with symbols.

Assessment

☞ ❏Accurately identifies each location; distances.
❏Calculated correctly.
❏Shows two different routes to go from one place to another.

☞ ❏Map is neatly drawn.
❏Scale is correct.
❏Key uses five or more symbols.

Level 3 Activities

1. Students will work in pairs. Each pair will be given a state road map and will be given a list of 20 cities, small towns, tourist areas and bodies of water. Using the map scale, they will figure distances between each place and highlight their preferred route, visiting each place once. They will write a paragraph explaining their preferred route and will defend it with three or more logical reasons.
2. Each student will make a detailed grid map of a local shopping mall, including a scale, compass rose and a key with symbols.

Assessment

☞ ❏Accurately identifies each location.
❏Distances calculated correctly.
❏Logical explanation of why their route is preferred.
❏Has 3 or more reasons.
❏Has correct spelling, punctuation and grammar.

☞ ❏Map is neatly drawn.
❏Details of entire mall are included.
❏Scale and compass rose are accurate.
❏Key uses ten or more symbols.

Whole Class Culminating Activities

1. Students will return to the heterogeneous groups they were in during the whole class introductory activities. All will share and explain the maps they have made.
2. Students will invent and name an imaginary continent or island and draw a map of it including cardinal and intermediate directions, a scale, compass rose and key, and at least five towns, cities, waterways, or other interesting features.
3. All maps will be shared and explained to the whole class.

Assessment

☞ ❏Group cooperation and sharing.

☞ ❏Maps are neatly drawn.
❏Visually attractive.
❏All required elements.
❏Shows creative and original thinking.

☞ ❏Oral explanation is clear.
❏Corresponds to the map being displayed.

Tiered Lesson Plan: Paragraph Writing

Objectives or Standards

1. Students will write complete sentences beginning with capital letters and ending with correct punctuation.
2. Students will use the correct paragraph format with topic sentence, detail sentences and concluding sentence.

Whole Class Activities

1. Teacher will review what makes a good sentence, emphasizing capital letters, sentence structure and punctuation.

2. Teacher will demonstrate how a paragraph is constructed with topic sentence, detail sentences and a concluding sentence.

3. Class will brainstorm ideas for paragraph topics.

4. Class will pick one topic and together will write a paragraph on this topic using the board, chart paper or overhead.

Assessment

❑ All listening and asking questions as appropriate.

❑ All observing teacher's demonstration.

❑ All students participating.

Level 1 Activities

1. Students will choose a topic from the topics brainstormed by the class. Teacher will help them write a topic sentence. Each student will then write three detail sentences and a concluding sentence for the paragraph.

2. Students will edit their paragraphs with the help of the teacher.

3. Each student will draw a picture to illustrate his or her paragraph.

Assessment

☞ ❑ Has three detail sentences.
❑ All students participating.
❑ Has a concluding sentence.
❑ Sentences support the topic sentence.

☞ ❑ Sentences are complete.
❑ Correct spelling, punctuation and grammar.

☞ ❑ Picture is creative.
❑ Neatly done.
❑ Goes along with the paragraph.

Level 2 Activities

1. Each student will choose a topic from the topics brainstormed by the class. Each will write a paragraph with a topic sentence, four detail sentences and a concluding sentence.

2. Students will work with a partner to edit and revise their paragraphs.

3. Each student will draw a picture to illustrate his or her paragraph.

Assessment

☞ ❑Has a topic sentence.
❑Four detail sentences.
❑Concluding sentence that supports the topic sentence.

☞ ❑Sentences are complete.
❑Correct spelling, punctuation and grammar.

☞ ❑Picture is creative.
❑Neatly done.
❑Goes along with the paragraph.

Level 3 Activities

1. Each student will choose a topic from the topics brainstormed by the class. Each will write two or three paragraphs on the topic, each with a topic sentence, detail sentences and a concluding sentence.

2. Students will edit and revise their own paragraphs.

3. Each student will draw a picture to illustrate his or her paragraphs.

Assessment

☞ ❑Each paragraph has a topic sentence.
❑Detail sentences and a concluding sentence supports the topic sentence.
❑All paragraphs are about the topic.

☞ ❑Sentences are complete.
❑Correct spelling, punctuation and grammar.

☞ ❑Picture is creative.
❑Neatly done.
❑Goes along with the topic chosen.

Whole Class Culminating Activities

1. Students will work in heterogeneous groups reading their paragraphs and sharing their illustrations.

2. Students will make a list of "Hints for Good Editing" and put it on a poster. Posters from all groups will be hung around the room for future reference.

Assessment

☞ ❑Group participation.
❑Ability to read own writing.
❑Clear presentation.
❑Ability to listen to others.

☞ ❑Follows Poster criteria card.
❑Has at least five suggestions for good editing.

Tiered Lesson Plan: Simple Machines

Objectives or Standards

1. To identify simple machines and learn how they work.
2. To explain the uses of various simple machines.
3. To compare and contrast various types of simple machines.
4. To learn ways to classify objects, communicate with others and to make inferences.

Whole Class Activities

1. Read <u>The Three Pigs and the Scientific Wolf</u> (Pieces of Learning, publisher) to the class. Do activities and worksheets as desired.

2. Discuss characteristics and types of simple machines and list on board.

3. In small heterogeneous groups, have students cut out pictures of everyday items and classify them according to what kind of simple machine they are, using inferences if they are not sure of the classification.

4. Share in large group with the class making a mural of simple machines combining all of their pictures.

Assessment

❏All listening and asking questions as appropriate.
❏Worksheets completed if assigned.

❏Characteristics and types of machines listed are correct.

❏Pictures of various types of machines are included.
❏Discussion of how to make inferences if you aren't sure of classification.

❏Mural shows classifications clearly.
❏Machines are classified correctly.
❏All groups are included.

Level 1 Activities

1. Choose one type of simple machine: lever, wheel, screw, spring, ramp or pulley. Design your own use for this type of machine. Make a model of it.

2. Draw a diagram showing how your machine works.

3. Write three or four sentences explaining your machine and the diagram.

Assessment

❏Model uses one type of simple machine.
❏Model is accurate and sturdy.

❏Diagram is neatly done.
❏Clearly shows how machine works.

❏Machine and diagram are explained accurately.
❏Sentences are complete.
❏Correct spelling, punctuation and grammar.

Level 2 Activities

1. Choose two simple machines from the following list: lever, wheel, screw, spring, ramp or pulley. Invent a machine that uses two of these simple machines or make a model of one that already exists.

2. Draw a diagram showing how your machine works.

3. Write two paragraphs explaining how and why your machine works as it does. Include knowledge of scientific principles.

☞ ❏Invented machine or model of existing machine uses two simple machines from the list.

☞ ❏Diagram is neatly done.
❏Clearly shows how machine works.

☞ ❏How and why the machine works are explained accurately.
❏Includes knowledge of scientific principles.
❏Sentences are complete.
❏Correct spelling, punctuation and grammar.

Level 3 Activities

1. Find a machine that combines wheels, pulleys and gears. Write an explanation of the function of each of these in the machine you have chosen.

2. Make a model and a diagram showing how the machine works.

3. Write four paragraphs summarizing the scientific principles involved in the workings of each with a concluding paragraph about the uses of your chosen machine.

Assessment

☞ ❏Chosen machine combines wheels, pulleys and gears.
❏Explains function of each.

☞ ❏Model and diagram are accurate representations.
❏Neatly done.
❏Clearly show how the machine works.

☞ ❏Scientific principles clearly explained for each of the three machines.
❏Uses of each machine are discussed.
❏Sentences are complete.
❏Correct spelling, punctuation and grammar.

Whole Class Culminating Activities

1. Students will share their models.

2. Students will invent a class machine that combines all six types of simple machines.

3. Use activities as desired from Primary Education Thinking Skills 3 (pages 76-122) on inventing new machines (Pieces of Learning, publisher).

Assessment

☞ ❏Group participation.
❏Clear presentation.
❏Ability to listen to others.

☞ ❏Combines all types of simple machines.
❏Entire class participates.

☞ ❏Assess as directed in book.

Tiered Lesson Plan: Soil

Objectives or Standards

1. Understand soil concepts and differentiate the properties of soil.
2. Analyze the ability of soil to support the growth of many plants.
3. Identify various types of soil.
4. Understand the process of composting.

Whole Class Activities

1. Read aloud pages 1-13 in the book <u>Dirt</u> by Steve Tomecek (Jump Into Science Series, National Geographic Society, Washington, D.C.)

2. Divide into 4 heterogeneous groups. Assign each group a type of soil: Gravel, Sand, Silt and Clay. Each group will make an illustrated poster showing color and texture along with information about their assigned type of soil and what can grow there.

3. Read aloud pages 14-25 in the book <u>Dirt</u>.

Assessment

☞ ❑All students paying attention.
❑Discussion and questions as book is read.

☞ ❑Illustration shows soil type, texture and color.
❑Written facts about soil.
❑Representative plants for soil type shown.

☞ ❑All students participating.

Level 1 Activities

1. Draw a detailed picture or diagram of earthworms and insects in the soil. Include labels of what you draw.

2. List at least five benefits of what these creatures do.

Assessment

☞ ❑Earthworms, insects and habitat clearly shown.
❑Clearly labeled.

☞ ❑Accurate list of five benefits.

Level 2 Activities

1. Create a flowchart showing the steps in creating humus from a compost pile.

2. List and analyze the functions of at least five living organisms in a compost pile.

Assessment

☞ ❑Steps clearly shown.
❑Accurate order.
❑Neat.
❑Well organized.

☞ ❑Five organisms listed.
❑Functions described.
❑Relationships to one another shown.

Level 3 Activities

1. List the advantages and disadvantages of gravel, sand, clay and silt when growing plants.

☞ ❑Accurate advantages and disadvantages of each listed.

2. Write a letter to a developer of a new subdivision in your area. Explain the importance of soil and give your suggestions about the best uses for the soil on the land to be developed.

☞ ❑Correct letter form.
❑Accurate spelling.
❑Accurate grammar.
❑Suggestions show knowledge of types of soil and their uses.

Whole Class Culminating Activities

Assessment

1. Share products and ideas from leveled activities.

☞ ❑All listen and participate.

2. Using clear plastic 2-liter bottles, make model soil ecosystems. (See pgs. 30-31 in the book Dirt.)

☞ ❑Followed directions for making model.
❑Different soils used.
❑Observations recorded.

3. Sing "Diggin' in the Dirt" by Peggosus (Boston Skyline recording). Make up movements to the words. Download and play song at
http://artists.iuma.com/IUMA/Bands/Peggosus/

☞ ❑All participate in singing and movements.

Tiered Lesson Plan: Southeast Asia

Objectives or Standards

1. To know basic information about the lands and people of Southeast Asia.
2. To explore information about one Southeast Asian country in depth.
3. To understand difficulties new immigrants from Southeast Asia might face in the United States.
4. To explore and understand positive aspects of Southeast Asian cultures within a multicultural society.

Whole Class Activities

1. On a map, label each Southeast Asian country. Indicate principal bodies of water, major cities and important landforms.

2. As a class, read a story, legend or fable from a Southeast Asian country. Depending on available resources, all students can read the same story or different stories. Each student will draw a web showing the plot, characters and main ideas.

3. Collect newspaper and magazine articles about Southeast Asia. Put on the bulletin board with a map to indicate locations of stories.

4. Have immigrants from one or more Southeast Asian countries come and speak to the class, telling about their culture and experiences.

Assessment

☞ ❑Follows Map criteria card.
❑All required items labeled.
❑Placed correctly on map.

☞ ❑Web shows plot, characters and main ideas.
❑Discussion of how the story reflects the culture and ideas of the country it takes place in.

☞ ❑Stories represent a variety of Southeast Asian countries.
❑A balance of positive stories if there are negative stories.
❑Correct locations on map.

☞ ❑All students listen to speakers.
❑Ask questions.
❑Participate in class discussion.

Level 1 Activities

1. Make a T-shirt showing a scene from a Southeast Asian country. Print a positive slogan above, beneath or around the picture.

2. Interview someone who has immigrated from a Southeast Asian country in the past decade. Summarize his/her views about the U.S. and about the immigration experience.

3. Each student will choose one country in Southeast Asia and develop and informational chart that has the following information: Major Cities, Natural Resources, Government, Important Landforms and Unusual Facts.

Assessment

☞ ❑T-shirt has a recognizable scene from a Southeast Asian country.
❑Slogan is clear and appropriate.

☞ ❑Interviewed a person from Southeast Asia.
❑Written summary is clear.
❑Shows views about America and the immigration experience.

☞ ❑Follows Chart criteria card.
❑Has all five categories.
❑Accurate information.

Level 2 Activities

1. Write and illustrate a poem that reflects your feelings about the diversity of the American population due to the immigration of many people from Southeast Asia.
2. Interview someone who fought in the Vietnam War. Do a five minute monologue or write a two page memoir of the war from his or her point of view.
3. Choose one country in Southeast Asia. Compare and contrast everyday life, boundaries, customs and government in 1945 and today. Show your findings and conclusions on some type of a visual.

Assessment

☞ ❑Poem is at least 10 lines long.
❑Shows feelings about diversity.
❑Illustration goes along with message of poem.
☞ ❑Interview questions are appropriate for getting needed information.
❑Monologue or memoir is correct length.
❑Reflects both information and feelings.
☞ ❑Focuses on one country.
❑Accurate information about 1945 and the present.
❑Visual clearly shows information and conclusions.

Level 3 Activities

1. With a classmate, design a board game or card game about Southeast Asia. Include ways to teach about the history, geography, people and culture of the region.
2. Interview an immigrant from Southeast Asia and an immigrant from Mexico or South America. Give them the same questions to answer. Compare and contrast their answers, then write "My View of America" from each of their points of view.
3. Choose 1 Southeast Asian country. Figure out the ratio of the population living in the cities compared to the population in rural areas in 1950, 1960, 1970, 1980, 1990 and 2000. Write a two page report discussing your conclusions and your predictions for the future based on this information.

Assessment

☞ ❑Follows Game criteria card.
❑Has facts about Southeast Asian history, geography, people and culture.

☞ ❑Interview questions are appropriate for getting needed information.
❑Written work shows similarities and differences in point of view between the two cultures.

☞ ❑Report is at least two pages long.
❑Has accurate facts for all years required.
❑Contains both conclusions and predictions for the future.
❑Has correct spelling.
❑Has correct grammar and punctuation.

Whole Class Culminating Activities

1. In small mixed-ability groups, students will share work done in leveled groups.

2. The class will design a new flag for the entire region of Southeast Asia. The flag should include designs and symbols important to the region.

3. The class will view a video that takes place in Southeast Asia. After viewing, they will list things in the movie that are true for the region and those things that are fiction.

Assessment

☞ ❑Group participation.
❑Ability to share information.
❑Ability to listen to others.

☞ ❑Flag is colorful.
❑Neatly drawn.
❑Contains designs and symbols significant for Southeast Asia.

☞ ❑List uses knowledge and understandings gained from this unit of study.

Tiered Lesson Plan: Westward Movement - Pioneer LIfe

Objectives or Standards

1. Students will understand reasons for the westward movement and some of the problems pioneers faced.
2. Students will know the various means of transportation used during the westward movement.
3. Students will be able to explain aspects of the social and economic impact of the westward movement.
4. Students will understand what life was like for pioneer families.
5. Students will discuss an historical novel and compare it to other information about the same time period.

Whole Class Activities

1. Read and discuss the book <u>Sarah, Plain and Tall</u> (or another similar book set in pioneer times).
2. View the video of the same story.
3. Brainstorm a list of similarities and differences between the video and the book. Discuss the advantages and disadvantages of books and videos as ways to tell a story.
4. Discuss what has been learned about pioneer life and the Westward Movement from reading this book.
5. Read background information about this topic from textbook or other sources.

Assessment

❑All students read book and watch video.

❑As desired, oral discussion, written questions or notes can be used to assess understanding.

❑List has similarities and differences.

❑All participate in discussion.

❑Notes or outline of basic information.

❑Accuracy of information.

Level 1 Activities

1. Each student will create a poster advertising a trip west and telling why people should go.

2. Each student will make a model of a Conestoga wagon, label important parts and write a description of how it was used to transport families to the west.

Assessment

☞ ❑Follows Poster criteria card.
❑Clearly shows reasons for going west.
❑Uses persuasive language.

☞ ❑Follows Model criteria card.
❑Important parts labeled.
❑Historically accurate.
❑Description is clear.
❑Explains use of wagon.

Level 2 Activities

1. Each student will write an editorial explaining at least three reasons why people should move west.

2. Each student will make a diorama depicting some form of transportation used during the westward movement. Include details regarding dates, how the land looked and the location depicted in the diorama.

Assessment

☞ ❑Reasons are logical.
❑Uses persuasive language.
❑Correct spelling.
❑Punctuation and grammar.

☞ ❑Follows Diorama criteria card.
❑Type of transportation clearly shown.
❑Includes accurate dates, scenery and location.

Level 3 Activities

1. Students will work in pairs to research three problems experienced by the pioneers moving west. They will make a chart listing Problem, Cause, and Possible Solution.

2. Each student will make a map showing one of the routes used by the pioneers as they traveled from the east to the west. Each will research to find out the various forms of transportation used on this route, and include this information on the map using a different symbol for each type.

Assessment

☞ ❑Follows Chart criteria card.
❑Historically accurate.
❑Shows good reasoning.
❑Indicates problem, cause and solutions.

☞ ❑Map is neatly drawn.
❑Route and types of transport are historically accurate.
❑Symbols show types of transportation used.

Whole Class Culminating Activities

1. Each student will write a journal of a trip west, pretending to be a pioneer sometime during the years 1865-1900. Each journal will have a map and at least ten different entries.

2. In heterogeneous groups of four, students will read their journals to each other and discuss different viewpoints of pioneer life.

3. Using information from the journals and other information learned in the unit, each group will write and illustrate a 10 page book about pioneer life to be read to a kindergarten or first grade class.

Assessment

☞ ❑Journal has 10 entries.
❑Is historically accurate.
❑Includes details of pioneer life.
❑Written in first person.

☞ ❑Group discussion and cooperation.

☞ ❑Follows Illustrated Booklet criteria card.
❑Details of pioneer life are shown.
❑Accurate information.

How To Write Tiered Lessons And Units

Writing tiered lessons and units can be challenging. Below are some steps to guide your planning. Use the blank Tiered Lesson form on the next page on the *Activities and Assessment* CD to write your own Tiered Lesson or Unit.

____1. Establish which standards, objectives, knowledge or skills all students need to know at the end of this lesson or unit. Use your state's standards documents to guide you.

____2. Think about activities you have done with students in the past to reach these standards or objectives. Make a list of all you can think of.

____3. Add more activities to your list as you brainstorm with other teachers or get ideas from the textbook or other resources.

____4. Decide which of these are appropriate learning activities for all students. These will become your whole class activities.

____5. Some of the activities on your list will most likely be easier than others. Put an indication of the level or tier you think each activity might be. Consider your class and decide on how many levels you need to have. You usually will have two or three levels, but occasionally you may have four levels.

____6. Think about ways to expand or extend the easier activities so they will be challenging for higher ability students and ways to simplify the more difficult activities so that your struggling students can do them successfully.

____7. Look carefully at your list of activities. Many times you will have more activities than your students could possibly do given the amount of time you have for the unit. Decide which activities are essential and which could be eliminated if necessary. You may want to save a few of the activities to use with students at any level who finish their work before others.

____8. Check again to make sure all activities will lead to students learning and mastering the standards and objectives.

____9. Make certain that activities at all levels are engaging and interesting. Nothing discourages achievement faster than students thinking that the other group is the one with the fun, interesting or enjoyable activity while the learning activity they have been assigned is not.

____10. Write your unit or lesson plan using the Tiered Lesson Plan form found on pages 151-152. You can also find this form on the *Activities and Assessment* CD.

____11. Plan daily lessons based on your Tiered Lesson or Unit plan.

____12. As you would with any lesson or unit, gather supplies and resources needed to do the activities.

Tiered Lesson Plan: Unit Planning Form

_____

Objectives or Standards

1.

2.

3.

4.

Whole Class Activities

Assessment

Level 1 Activities

Assessment

Level 2 Activities

Assessment

Level 3 Activities

Assessment

Whole Class Culminating Activities

Assessment

If you feel you are not creative enough to think of ways to differentiate activities, use the list below and fill in the blank with the appropriate content or subject matter. You will be surprised how this will start your creativity flowing! These are suggestions to get you started. You will think of many more.

Make a model of _____.

Develop a picture dictionary on the topic of _____.

Draw a map showing _____.

Create a brochure about _____.

Write a journal from the point of view of _____.

Create Jeopardy questions about _____.

Make a Venn Diagram comparing and contrasting _____.

Make picture postcards showing _____.

Write a poem about _____.

Write an editorial expressing your opinion about _____.

Do a written report on _____.

Tape a radio report telling about _____.

Write a myth or legend explaining _____.

Make a diorama showing _____.

Produce a video news report about _____.

Write an epilogue to _____.

Role play _____.

Write a letter describing _____.

Create song lyrics and music to tell about _____.

Draw a comic strip about _____.

Make a time line showing _____.

Construct an information cube with the following information on it:
_____.

Make a speech about _____.

Construct puppets and put on a puppet show about _____.

Write a diary entry dated _____.

Develop a pro and con chart about _____.

Design a game to teach about _____.

Make a flow chart showing _____.

Interview _____, creating at least 5 interview questions.

Search the Internet for information about _____.

Do a PowerPoint presentation on _____.

Make a crossword puzzle about _____.

Do an oral report using visuals about _____.

Make a collage of _____.

Explain _____ in paragraph form.

Design a symbol of _____.

Write a short story about _____.

Design a T-shirt showing _____.

Make a word search about _____.

Make an illustrated booklet of _____.

Design a study guide for _____.

Generate a graph to show _____.

Conduct an email interview with _____.

Debate with a classmate _____.

Make a mobile showing _____.

Do a slide show on the computer about _____.

Use a digital camera to _____.

Make a poster showing _____.

Make a scrapbook of _____.

Design a bookmark about _____.

Create a mural showing _____.

Write a shape story about _____.

Make a chart to show _____.

Do a scale drawing of _____.

Arrange a display showing _____.

Do a sand painting for _____.

Create a mosaic depicting _____.

Lead a class discussion on _____.

Write and direct a one-act play about _____.

Read a book about _____.

Evaluate the effect of _____.

Design a plan to _____.

Do a concept map or web showing _____.

Using Learning Contracts to Structure Differentiated Activities

A learning contract is an agreement between a student and the teacher (and sometimes the parent) that states the tasks or activities the student will do. Learning contracts often have rules and guidelines, due dates and options for student choices in assignments. This is one approach to use when students do independent study or an individualized assignment in a differentiated classroom.

All learning contracts should have some type of rules or guidelines. Included in these might be:

• The amount and level of work that is required

• The due date for the assignment or assignments

• Where the student is allowed to go within the classroom or school when working on the learning contract

• Where and how to get help

• When and how formative assessments will be used before the final project or assignment is turned in

• When the teacher will check ongoing work and conference with the student

• How much adult assistance is allowed

• How the activities will be assessed or graded

The Tic-Tac-Toe Activities, *Teaching Tools* Individualized Lesson Plans and the leveled activities in the Tiered Lesson/Unit Plans can all be structured into learning contracts. Use them if it makes your classroom management easier or if it helps organize and focus your students.

In addition to using a contract in this manner, below are additional approaches using a learning contract.

1. Use learning contracts when a student wants to study an area of special interest and needs some structure in order to do it. Example 1 is a learning contract for a first grader who had just returned from Sea World and was interested in studying Whales. This contract is simple and easy to understand. The activities are suggested by three verbs understandable to young children: *Making*, *Writing* and *Doing*. This contract works very well with students in grades K-3.

2. Use learning contracts when the entire class is studying a certain topic and you want to give some structure for the study yet also give students choices with appropriate levels of challenge. Example 2 is an example of a tiered learning contract used by a class as they studied Ancient Egypt. It is tiered because it offers student choice in the levels of the Taxonomy.

Give all students the contract. Allow individual input and choices about the activities they would do and at what levels of Bloom's Taxonomy they would complete them.

The Learning Contracts are on the *Activities and Assessments* CD.

Learning Contract — Example 1

Name _____

I want to learn about _____ **Whales** _____

Materials I will use:

Books from Sea World about whales _____

Pictures, brochures and postcards _____

Computer software about marine mammals _____

Rules I will follow:

1. *I will work on this contract while sitting in my seat at school.*

2. *I will talk to only one person at a time about my topic.*

3. *I will work on the assignment at school and at home.*

I will show what I have learned by:

Making _____ *a whale model* _____

Writing _____ *a whale story* _____

Doing _____ *a report about whales for my class using my pictures*

I will finish this by _____ (date)

Student _____

Teacher _____

Parent _____

Learning Contract for Younger Students

Name _____

I want to learn about _____

Materials I will use:

_____

_____

_____

Rules I will follow:

1. _____

2. _____

3. _____

I will show what I have learned by:

Making _____

Writing _____

Doing _____

I will finish this by _____ (date)

Student _____

Teacher _____

Parent _____

Learning Contract — Example 2

Name _____

Topic _____Ancient Egypt_____

Resources:

Print and Internet resources are listed here by the student before beginning
the activities.

Rules I will follow while working on this contract:

    1. *I will keep a log of my work each day.*

    2. *I will come to class with materials needed to work on my learning contract*
activities.

    3. *I will not disturb others.*

I will show what I have learned by: (Bloom's Taxonomy verbs)

*Describing_____*a typical day for a student in Ancient Egypt*

*Illustrating_____*a what a village along the Nile River looks like*

*Summarizing *the different roles and jobs the poeple had in Ancient Egypt*

**Designing_____*a typical Egyptian Pyramid*

**Critiquing_____*the pros and cons of Egyptian embalming methods*

**Analyzing_____*similarities and differences between Ancient Egypt and the USA*__

I will do this by: _____(date)

Student _____

Teacher _____

* Bloom's Taxonomy lower level objectives

** Bloom's Taxonomy higher level objectives

Learning Contract

Name _____

Topic _____

Resources:

Rules I will follow while working on this contract:

I will show what I have learned by:

_____   _____
(Bloom's Taxonomy Verb)

_____   _____
(Bloom's Taxonomy Verb)

_____   _____
(Bloom's Taxonomy Verb)

I will do this by: _____(date)

Student _____

Teacher _____

Resources for Further Study

Betts, George and Kercher, Jolene, <u>Autonomous Learner Model</u>, Greeley, CO, ALPS Publishing, 1999.

Chapman, Carolyn and Gregory, G.H., <u>Differentiated Instructional Strategies: One Size Doesn't Fit All</u>, Thousand Oaks, CA, Corwin Press, 2002.

Coil, Carolyn, <u>Encouraging Achievement</u>, Marion, IL, Pieces of Learning, 1999.

Coil, Carolyn, <u>Motivating Underachievers</u>, Revised and expanded edition, Marion, IL, Pieces of Learning, 2001.

Coil, Carolyn, <u>Teaching Tools for the 21st Century</u>, Marion, IL, Pieces of Learning, 2000.

Coil, Carolyn and Merritt, Dodie, <u>Solving the Assessment Puzzle</u>, Marion, IL, Pieces of Learning, 2001.

Delisle, Jim and Lewis, Barbara, <u>The Survival Guide for Teachers of Gifted Kids</u>, Minneapolis, MN, Free Spirit Publishing, 2003.

Gardner, Howard, <u>Multiple Intelligences: The Theory in Practice</u>, New York, NY, Basic Books, 1993.

Heacox, Diane, <u>Differentiating Instruction in the Regular Classroom</u>, Minneapolis, MN, Free Spirit Publishing, 2002.

Kingore, Bertie, <u>Differentiation: Simplified, Realistic and Effective</u>, Austin, TX, Professional Associates, 2003.

Merritt, Dodie, <u>Independent Study</u>, Marion, IL, Pieces of Learning, 2002.

Nichols, Thomson, Wolfe and Merritt, <u>Primary Education Thinking Skills</u>, Marion, IL, 2000.

Polette, Nancy, <u>The Research Book for Gifted Programs K-8</u>, Revised edition, Marion, IL, Pieces of Learning, 2001.

Smutny, Joan, <u>Differentiated Instruction</u>, Fastback series #506, Bloomington, IN, Phi Delta Kappa, 2003.

Tomlinson, Carol Ann, <u>The Differentiated Classroom</u>, Alexandria, VA, Association for Supervision and Curriculum Development, 1999.

Winebrenner, Susan, <u>Teaching Gifted Kids in the Regular Classroom</u>, Revised and Expanded edition, Minneapolis, MN, Free Spirit Publishing, 2001.